Balancing & Blending Better Together

The
WILL of
a MAN &
The WAY of
a WOMAN

ROBERT & PAMELA CROSBY

SHILOH RUN PRESS

An Imprint of Barbour Publishing, Inc.

Member of the
Evangelical Christian
Publishers Association

PRAISE FOR *THE WILL OF A MAN &*
THE WAY OF A WOMAN

"Robert and Pamela have given us a view on marriage that we have not seen before. I know that this will bring each reader a new understanding on how to have a successful and godly marriage. I highly recommend this book."

—Matthew Barnett, CEO of The Dream Center

"Robert and Pamela's heartfelt, vulnerable stories will resonate deeply with your own realities and connect you to the psychological, emotional, and spiritual principles that will surely redefine and revolutionize your understanding of God's design in your relationship with one another."

—Molly Godzich, Executive Director of
the National Association of Marriage Enhancement

" 'These two shall become one!' *The Will & The Way* principle does more than help us understand *marriage*; as husbands and wives, it helps us understand *ourselves* and how to take major steps in the journey toward *oneness*!"

—Dr. Samuel Rodriguez, President of NHCLC/Conela

"Honest, candid, biblical, relevant, helpful, and hopeful! We hope all couples choose to bend their WILL and make a WAY to read TOGETHER the Crosby's terrific new book: *The Will of a Man & the Way of a Woman.*"

—Pam and Bill Farrel, Authors of 45 books including the bestselling
Men Are Like Waffles, Women Are Like Spaghetti

"Robert and Pamela Crosby masterfully address the challenging task of every marriage—two becoming one. . . . *The Will of a Man & the Way of a Woman* is an extraordinary book that will help married couples enjoy the beauty of balancing and blending better together."

—Guillermo and Milagros Aguayo, Founders,
Salvemos a la Familia, Lima, Peru

"The Crosbys offer us handles and roadmaps to understand men and women, especially in a world that lacks clarity. Doubtless, the genders share equality, but they also share diversity. This book helps us all understand how males and females both magnetically draw and repel each other and how to leverage that magnetism brilliantly. I recommend this book."

—Tim Elmore, President, GrowingLeaders.com

"This book is a must-read on building relationships. Few resources compare to the practical lessons Robert and Pamela Crosby share about building a lifetime of togetherness."

—Dr. Kent Ingle, President, Southeastern University

"Great authors are known for their ability to write precise words that contain a priceless wealth of wisdom to enrich their reading audience. I thoroughly enjoyed the masterful thoughts, life experiences, and wise principles of Robert and Pamela Crosby skillfully recorded and shared in this book. A must-read for men and women who desire to reap the rewards of an endless relational treasure to be passed down for a lasting family legacy."

—Dr. Joaquin G. Molina, Pastor and Author

"Over time, every Christian couple experiences misunderstandings and frustration that lead to feelings of isolation and resentment. What to do? Dive into this book for scripture-based, practical solutions offered by a caring, experienced couple who live their insights. You'll get pulled right in, finding principles for the mind, healing for the heart, and hope for the spirit that help guide a couple to the wholeness Christ intends!"

—Dr. Dan and Kate Montgomery, Authors of *The Self Compass: Charting Your Personality in Christ*

"The principles in this book illuminate truths about men and women that everyone needs to know to build a healthy marriage. The Crosbys have taught us a lot about marriage through their wisdom and example. These concepts laid the groundwork for how we develop and grow our passion for one another now and have given us a solid foundation on which to build our relationship. If you're married, engaged, or desire to learn about healthy relationships, you NEED to read this book."

—Taylor and Kristen Wilkerson, Pastors, Trinity Church-Harlem, NYC

"Robert and Pamela Crosby do not mince words in getting to the heart of what it means to grow a successful marriage. They blend personal illustrations, reality, and wise practice. They pull no punches! *The Will of a Man & the Way of a Woman* is an invitation to a 'relational oneness' through understanding, practice, and enjoyment. This book is for every counselor, educator, church leader, and married man and woman."

—Dr. Robert E. Cooley, President Emeritus, Gordon-Conwell Theological Seminary

"Whether you are married for a short time or have years to reflect upon, Robert and Pamela bring a needed conversation to the forefront of marriage today in their book, *The Will of a Man & the Way of a Woman*. Both come to this topic with 30 years of marriage and many years of speaking to couples and engaging with the next generation of couples who are college students. The idea of our marriage relationship drawing us together and then pulling us apart based on how a husband and a wife function in marriage is a gift to be understood, not a force to wrestle with. I am impressed, motivated, and drawn to the way that Robert and Pamela share openly from their lives and clarify throughout the book how men and women are different by design emotionally and spiritually and how we can pinpoint while valuing the other's approach and come out better as a couple. It is a book I'll recommend for years to come to new and established married couples."

—Blythe Daniel, Literary Agent, The Blythe Daniel Agency, Inc.

Lords of creation, whom your ladies rule—
The world's great masters, when you're out of school—
Learn the brief moral of our evening's play:

Man has his will—but woman has her way!

Oliver Wendell Holmes Sr.
The Atlantic Journal, 1858

To
Bob and Beverly Crosby
and
David and Shirley Krist
(a.k.a., Dad and Mom)

We honor you for choosing to live the married life—
for surrendering your wills and yielding your ways to God
and to each other for sixty years and running. . .

Contents

Introduction: The Will of a Man and the Way
   of a Woman 9

Part I: Balancing: *Understanding* the Will and the Way

Chapter 1: The Note 19

Chapter 2: When His *Will* Gets in Her *Way*. 33

Chapter 3: Something in the Way: His Struggle
   and Hers................................. 47

Chapter 4: When Parents Know, Children Grow 59

Part II: Bending: *Practicing* the Will and the Way

Chapter 5: Bending Your Will, Finding the Way 73

Chapter 6: My Way or the Highway! 87

Chapter 7: Getting His Attention: The Ultimate
   "Power" Tool 103

Chapter 8: The Peacekeeper and the Truth-Teller 113

Chapter 9: Attunement: Listening with
   Your Third Ear 129

Chapter 10: A Parent's Path: The Best Way
to Lead Will. 143

Part III: Blending: *Enjoying* the Will and the Way

Chapter 11: The Teaming Couple 161

Chapter 12: What Men Want Most!. 175

Chapter 13: What Women Deeply Desire! 187

Chapter 14: Where There's a Will. 203

Chapter 15: The Will and the Way. . .
in the Bedroom 219

Chapter 16: Restoring Marriage: Living God's Will,
God's Way 233

Acknowledgments. 247

Schedule an Event in Your Area with Robert
and Pamela Crosby. 250

Endnotes 251

INTRODUCTION

THE WILL OF A MAN AND THE WAY OF A WOMAN

There's something about the *will* of a man and the *way* of a woman. You can feel it at work in your relationship. It's like two magnets side by side that are powerfully drawn together at once; but just flip one of them over, and those magnetic poles can actually repel or push each other away. It is ironic that the one we love and to whom we are so deeply drawn can at times conversely and even unknowingly push us away.

Sound familiar?

We all long for a place in which we can be ourselves, our true selves. Understanding more about the will of a man and the way of a woman has helped us get our heads and hearts around the potential and the challenges of making a marriage work. It has enhanced the magnetic draw we feel and helped us better understand the times when we push each other away.

While many people are waiting longer to get married today, a recent *Time* magazine article affirms that most millennials want to get married and that divorce rates have, perhaps surprisingly, been dropping among all ages since the 1980s.[1] Thus, a higher percentage of marriages are lasting or lasting longer. The one exception, however, is older people. In fact, divorce rates among these groups are up, having doubled among people fifty and older in the past two decades. This same article noted that due to technology and sociological changes, "in many ways, getting married is now easier than it has ever been. But [for many] staying married, and doing so happily, is more difficult."[2]

So with this in mind, perhaps now is a great time to take a fresh look at your marriage, and your relationships in general, with the opposite sex. Maybe that is exactly why you picked up this book. As you walk with us for a few chapters on the path of the will of a man and the way of a woman, take time to consider your relationship, what you are learning about yourself and the one you love. To assist you in taking a fresh look, you will find questions at the end of each chapter that you can use in a few ways: (1) to ask yourself, (2) to discuss with your partner, and/or (3) to discuss with a small group of other couples.

THE PRINCIPLE

The principle of *The Will of a Man and the Way of a Woman* is about an inner motivation that exists at the core of our souls. It basically says this: while the *will* of a man compels him to act on *the strengths* he feels he can offer his wife, the *way* of a woman compels her to act out of *the understanding* she feels she can offer her husband, drawing them both into a relational oneness. The principle of the will and the way is alive and at work in marriages, in parenting, and in all kinds of relationships between males and females.

When the insight of the will and the way began to unfold for us in our marriage, it became the GPS in our relationship. We have turned to this relational guide many times since, often several times a day, to navigate steep hills and sharp turns.

The Bible's earliest descriptions of the connection of

men and women describe the palpable "draw" between them. For instance, when we read the account of the moment Adam first laid eyes on Eve in all her unclothed glory, we can feel the magnetism and the motivation. His poignant first words said it all: "'This is now. . .flesh of my flesh'" (Genesis 2:23 NIV).

In other words, Adam was saying to his newly introduced counterpart, *"You are a part of me, and I am a part of you."* These words drip with vulnerability and intimacy.

A pattern of magnetic attraction was established in this first account of a relationship between a man and a woman—one that has played out again and again billions of times since, even in our own lives. The earliest description of man and woman in scripture is a vivid depiction of a connection—a connection between a man and a woman to each another.

> *[For this reason] shall a man* leave *his father and his mother, and shall* cleave *unto his wife: and they shall be one flesh.*
> (Genesis 2:24 KJV, emphasis added)

Love brought the man and the woman together. However, once sin and selfishness entered the scene, fear clearly pushed them apart. Intimacy was interrupted. The dilemma and relational drama continues to this day in our relationships. The magnetic push and pull. The drawing near to love, the pushing away of fear—exploring the garden of intimacies at times, and at others, running away from God, from each other, and even from ourselves.

The principle of the will of a man and the way of a woman has helped us view each other more realistically and graciously. It has tempered our expectations of each other.

Honestly, when we began to recognize it, we felt as if it cracked a code of confusion we had too often wrestled with. The tumblers of the lock fell into place and opened a new level of closeness and trust between the two of us.

This book tells the story of our personal experiences and insights with the will and the way, including the strengths and struggles in our own marriage. So, be warned. We have tried not to pull any punches in this account. The stories are honest and direct. We have included some of our most satisfying discoveries about marriage as well as some of our most frustrating moments. Our hope is that they will inform, encourage, and support you in your relationship with your spouse and with the opposite sex in general.

Understanding more about the will of a man and the way of a woman has also strengthened our appreciation of each other's strengths and weaknesses, enhancing our ability to effectively communicate with each other. The oneness we have experienced as a result has reduced the stresses in our marriage, parenting, and work environments. Our prayer is that you will experience the same.

MARRIAGES AND MARATHONS

Some of the richest rewards or dividends of marriage do not come instantly but require a lifetime of effort. Research repeatedly shows that the investments people make in their spouses and their marriages over an extended period of time can reap deeply satisfying results. In fact, "new evidence keeps piling up that few things are as good for life, limb and liquidity as staying married."[3]

One Cornell University researcher surveyed seven hundred elderly people and found that 100 percent of them said at one point that their "long marriage was the best thing in their lives."[4] However, all of these couples also acknowledged that marriage is hard and requires intentional and consistent effort. Because of increased life expectancy, "until death do us part" is longer than ever before. In fact, marriage today can stretch from a wedding, having kids, putting them through school, and going into retirement, with decades yet to live together.

One of our favorite quotes is by Marcel Proust: "The real voyage of discovery consists not in seeking new landscapes but in having new eyes."[5] This insight is so fitting for marriage because it captures a major aspect of what it requires to grow a strong and fulfilling one. Understanding each other through the ups and downs of married life is a revelation. If we are open to growing, changing, and learning more about each other and what it means to love well, our eyes will be opened and our souls more fulfilled.

One of the nation's leading marriage researchers, Dr. John Gottman, found that older married couples "tend to behave like younger married couples [both inside and] outside the bedroom too."[6] In fact, surprisingly, the longer a couple stays together, the more a sense of kindness returns to their relationship. In essence, in later life the marriage once again takes on the characteristics of the couple's initial courtship.

The *last* thing we believe a marriage or a book about marriage ought to be is rigid and one-dimensional. This book and the principle it reveals do not provide a hard and fast binary definition of men and women that *always* applies to *all* men and *all* women at *all* times and in *all* the same ways. No. Such an idea would be ridiculous and all too formulaic.

In a world full of men and women wired with so many different personalities shaped both by their DNA and socialization, by nature and nurture, it would be foolish to paint men and women as mere monolithic groups. For people of faith, it would be even more foolish to overlook the insights, inspirations, and examples provided in God's Word (the Bible) that shed light on the image of God (the *Imago Dei*), His handiwork, and the unique and potentially complementary expressions of humankind represented in male and female forms.

> *When God created mankind, he made them in the likeness of God.* He created them male and female *and blessed them. And he named them "Mankind" when they were created.*
> (Genesis 5:1–2 NIV, emphasis added)

From the moment man was made out of the dust of the earth (Genesis 2:7) and the woman was made out of the man (vv. 21–22), God formed them with similar characteristics but with unique depths of purpose. They were formed to know and find their identities in Him and also to complement each other. Consider this:

> *And God blessed them. And God said to them,*

*"Be fruitful and multiply and fill the earth
and subdue it, and* have dominion *over the
fish of the sea and over the birds of the heavens
and over every living thing that moves on the
earth."*

(Genesis 1:28 ESV, emphasis added)

From the start men and women were designed by God to "have dominion" over the earth and "every living thing that moves" on it. But "dominion" is not about control; it is all about purpose—loving, caring, stewarding, and serving. While "dominion" for the male meant that the garden was a place he could *display his strength by applying his will* to working and serving, sin led to something else. Instead of "dominion," he too often turned it into control through *domination*. It became more about power than love (more on this in chapter 7). This has played out in so many ways throughout history and has hurt so many people, in particular women and children.

While "dominion" for the female originally meant that the garden was a place to *display and engage her beauty and discernment by applying her ways* to caring and nurturing, sin led to something else. Instead of "dominion," she too often turned it into control through *manipulation*. Again, as with Adam, power overruled the priority of love. This has been conveyed in so many ways since then throughout history and has damaged the mood and manner of so many homes and husbands and children.

The principle of the will and the way informs marriage but also other relationships. The negative uses of the will and the way also play out every day in the world of parenting, business, and politics. There have also been extremes in history where men and women have acted on these traits in terrifying ways that have led to much destruction.

But since Jesus came, we live in an age of grace. Jesus came "to seek and to save that which was lost" (Luke 19:10 KJV). He came to save men from their own stubborn will and to bring them back to His will and His plan. Jesus came to rescue women from their ways and waywardness and back to the everlasting way. Essentially, the quest is a return to Eden. Although it will never fully occur until the final day, we are called to seek it out and find ways to practice it every day.

There is something now absolutely liberating about the fact that the writer of Hebrews said, "Marriage is honourable in all, and the bed undefiled" (Hebrews 13:4 KJV—more about this in chapter 15, the "sex chapter"). Marriage is, in fact, an invitation for a man and a woman to rediscover love as originally intended to be given and enjoyed. Marriage is a "season pass" back to the garden of Eden. But it involves a passionate quest toward understanding, toward knowing and being known, of restoration and re-entering Eden-like intimacies together if but for a few incredible moments at a time. We call it the journey of the will of a man and the way of a woman—the journey toward oneness.

PART I

Balancing

Understanding the Will and the Way

CHAPTER 1
The Note

A great marriage is not when the "perfect couple" comes together. It is when an imperfect couple learns to enjoy their differences.
—Dave Meurer

I wondered if he would even see the note taped to the front door before he left home that morning. My day ahead was full of more dirty diapers, baskets of laundry, sinks full of dishes, and planning for the church event I was helping my husband with. No one asked how I was doing. No one called to check in on my day. I had no other family nearby to have coffee with. I was a young wife and a mom of two toddlers, struggling with more loneliness as a married woman than I ever had when single.

Each day Robert went to a job he thoroughly loved, worked with people who inspired him, and served in a role in which he found purpose and community. Each night he would come home, the front door would fling open, and you'd hear, "Daddy's home!" as the kids went shouting his praises as if Superman had just entered the house. By that time of day, I looked like I had been through a war zone.

Dinner usually included one of Robert's favorite dishes, and typically I prepared it while he enjoyed playtime with his two adorable little blond daughters. The moment dinner was over, the TV news went on. While the "king" caught up on world events, I bathed and put the girls to bed in hopes for just a little alone-with-him time to follow. After the fiftieth "Good night, Mommy," I was ready to cuddle and for some attention of my own.

Finally. The first quiet of my day would arrive.

The moments I looked forward to the most were moments with him, with my husband. Cuddle time on the couch with no little voices interrupting the latest romantic movie or bowl of ice cream or late-night cup of coffee (just because we could!) were among my favorite end-of-the-day highlights. But instead, as I entered the room, there he was. . .sprawled out on his favorite seven-foot couch, TV remote in hand, snoring like a monsoon. After all, *he* had worked hard all day. *He* was really tired. And soon after, *he* decided to go to bed.

Thus, came the abrupt end of a few hoped-for romantic moments, not to mention the only adult conversations I would have that day. No shared ice cream treat. No hugs. No real time together. No questions about my day.

The nights had become empty. But the rest of the week was always full—full of church events, youth pastor duties, band practices, training sessions, and before I knew it, a new week had begun that seemed somehow strangely similar to the last one. Honestly, more often than not, I felt more like a maid than a wife, but I kept telling myself it was okay because he was so happy in the world in which he was learning to succeed. After all, he was working so hard. I should be really grateful, right? I tried, but still I was so lonely—so lonely and becoming lonelier. I had never thought of myself one day feeling so lonely in marriage. Marriage and loneliness don't make a good couple. In fact, *lonely marriage* should be an oxymoron.

Should be.

What is a wife supposed to do with such feelings? I had so much that I wanted to say to him—so much I needed to say. But I didn't want to be *that* wife—the nagging wife who was never happy enough. Still, those emotions are a difficult thing to shake. Expectations are powerful. What I wanted to tell him was I needed more "him" in my life and more of "us." I wanted life to be like it was before the "I dos." I wanted a return to the spontaneous, the togetherness, the fewer responsibilities, the flirty responses, the tender touches, the getting "the butterflies" from just being in the same room, the love letters. Was it really all gone? Were we really going to grow or act old so soon? Was there something I could do? If so, what was it?

I was desperate to know.

I thought about it a lot.

I prayed about it.

What to do?

Someone once said, "Until the pain of remaining the same hurts more than the pain of changing, we tend to remain the same." Well, by this point my hurt had reached that place. I had to do something about it. At least I had to try something different.

One thing I had noticed and learned about Robert was that he learned a lot when he read books and manuals. I also noticed that the tone of my angry or whiny voice usually made him tune me right out. I knew I couldn't talk to girlfriends because we went to the same church and he was one of the spiritual leaders there, and that wouldn't go well for anyone. Plus, I was committed to protecting the intimate heart of our marriage and not allowing it to become the focus of girl-time chatter.

I hated feeling more like a housekeeper than a wife. I wanted to be the reason he came home. I wanted him to show me he still cared—really cared—about us. After weeks of wrestling with the issue and with myself, I did it. I wrote it down.

I sat at the table and began to pour my heart out in a way he might understand, on paper. I'd write something, read it, and then just throw it away and start over. Putting these feelings to paper took some practice. Finally, after several attempts, I had what I thought was a letter that spoke his language, while maybe not exactly mine. I tried to keep it short, using fewer words while keeping it to the point—honest but kind, respectful but truthful. Not easy.

I folded it neatly in a business envelope and taped it to the front door.

Then I waited.

Will he actually notice it? I bought him a new shirt and put it in a gift bag to accompany the note. Hopefully that would help him know I really cared. At least gifts had always gotten *my* attention. I wasn't exactly sure if they would *get* his. I didn't want him to get mad. I just wanted him to hear my heart.

With everything in place, I went to bed.

FINDING THE NOTE

The note taped to the front door I (Robert here) found the next morning was likely an ordinary to-do list from Pamela. Eager to head off to work while she was still sleeping, I slipped the note in my appointment book and set off to meet my day. I'd check the note later. Right now a schedule chock-full of other "responsibilities" wouldn't wait.

Somewhere around lunchtime, I noticed the note again. It had dropped out of my appointment book and lay on my desk, still untouched. When I opened it to take a quick look, the first sentence caught my attention: "Robert, I don't know what has happened to us." I decided I had better give it a full read.

The full note went something like this:

> Robert,
>
> I don't know what's happened to us. The life we're now living, from my view, is no life at all. At least, this is not what I ever thought life would become. It feels like you're more married to your work than you are to me. I'm confused. And I don't know what to do with all that it's causing me to feel.
>
> I've tried in lots of little ways to talk with you about this, but you just aren't hearing me. You're so creative at your work—I wish you would pour some of your creative energy into our home, into our children, into me.
>
> There are times I almost wish your preoccupation with your work were with another woman, so I could tell her to "bug off!"

Something in our relationship is dying, and I don't know what to do about it.

Now we have our second baby, and our girls need more than I can give them by myself. They need a daddy, and I need a husband. Robert, I don't know who to turn to.

Pamela

For the first time in months, Pamela's hurt and disappointment broke through my addictive self-consumption. I suddenly saw myself as a man busy living out his own interests. I felt alarmed by the desperate tone of her note.

Pamela had expressed her frustrations before. But I'd always viewed them as something she would eventually just "get over." This was different, maybe because I now connected the words in this note with the look I'd been seeing on her face—the look I'd been ignoring, a look of hopelessness and pain. Desperation.

I was embarrassed. While helping other people, had I totally overlooked my wife and family? What was I doing? How had I missed it? After all, I was *the pastor*. Two hundred teenagers and a couple dozen volunteer youth workers came to *me* for counsel and advice. Couples came to *me* for marriage counseling, and my files were full of ideas and prescriptions for enriching the marriage relationship.

After reading the note, I knew this was no yellow light. It was bright red.

When does the heart go out of a marriage? When does the connection between a man and a woman turn to conflict? What causes it? And what does it take to restore it?

Magnetic *Push* and *Pull*

Just as surely as there is a magnetic force that draws a man and a woman together, there is one that, conversely, can push them apart. Haven't we all watched it happen again and again in other couples' relationships and felt it in our own? Just like the two sides of a magnet, there is one side to the makeup of a man and a woman that is drawn together powerfully, romantically, and relationally. On the flip side, however, there is another aspect to the male and female composition that can forcefully repel them from each other, poles apart.

A young man and woman meet each other, fall in like, and then fall desperately in love. Most of their waking moments are filled with thoughts of the other. They rearrange their schedules just to have more time together, they ask each other questions constantly with great interest, they date, they talk on the phone, they send romantic cards, e-mails, or texts, they hold hands, and they look into each other's eyes. They pursue each other. The love they share and feel seems to be more than enough to overcome any differences they may discover. The magnetic pull draws them toward each other on multiple levels. From their hearts to their hormones, little else is on their minds.

Then something happens.

Somewhere along the way, the differences become more different than he or she ever thought possible. Driving hopes and dreams come to a halt. Expectations are exhausted. Hopes are suspended. Opinions have collided. Priorities have shifted. Desires have dissolved. The walls can seem insurmountable as the magnetic pull turns into magnetic push.

The *Will* and the *Way*

The magnetic principle at work that we are talking about is constantly drawing men and women together and then, all too often, driving them apart. It is a principle. We call it **the will** *of a man and* **the way** *of a woman*. It has to do with understanding the way God created men and women in the first place. Just one look and it is quite clear that we are designed differently, and the differences are more than just *anatomical*. An even closer look will reveal that men and women are different by design *emotionally* and even *spiritually* as well. Understanding and accepting the emotional and spiritual differences is the key to discovering the high purposes and roles in life God intended for both the man and the woman.

The bottom line of the will of a man and the way of a woman is this: *a man possesses a unique God-given propensity (i.e., drive) for exercising a* **strong will** *in life*. This is not to say that all men are "strong-willed"; rather, men are created with a powerful capacity for matters of volition (i.e., the will).

Conversely, a woman possesses a unique God-given propensity for understanding **the appropriate ways** *of life*. Similar to the observation of a man's will, a woman has a God-given, unique capacity for considering and responding to the deep emotional dimensions of life and to matters of understanding and discernment.

By now some of you are reading and already saying, "Whoa. Wait a minute. I think you have us reversed. In our case, the wife appears to be the one with the *will* and the husband with more interest in the *way*. Are we weird?"

The answer is yes. No, not yes that you are weird, but yes that there are anomalies to this principle that exist. Also, it is important not to confuse personality types, of which there are many, with the soul-centric motivations of the volitional and emotional capacities that undergird the design of men and women.

The will of a man and the way of a woman is a central, God-given, innate motivating drive that exists at the core of our souls. This goes beyond personality styles. When a couple understands the principle of *will* and *way* and accepts it, they are well on their way toward discovering the mysterious and magnetic oneness originally intended to be enjoyed in marriage.

TOWARD ONENESS

This brings us to the first relational practice of the will and the way and the first part of the book: *balancing*. Moving toward oneness with the person you love involves considering and understanding more of the differences expressed in the will of a man and the way of a woman. Understanding how your different strengths and weaknesses can work together in a complementary fashion is all about balance. This helps build a perspective that adds more purpose to your partnership.

We first began to see the principle of the will and the way at work in our own lives and marriage relationship, over and over again, from early on. Once we began to recognize it at work in a few places, it seemed we could see it almost everywhere. We began to notice it in our extended family and friends—all over the place. But what really caught our attention was when we observed it in one of the most beautiful and meaningful "couple stories" in the Bible—the story of Mary and Joseph.

That's right, the Gospel accounts of God announcing the incarnation to Mary, and then to Joseph, are so revealing—not just in what God said but in the *way* He said it. It is marvelous and also mysterious. An angel announced and revealed that their marriage would be the place where God's Son would soon emerge. No one in all of history ever received a more amazing, awe-inspiring, or life-altering announcement than this one. Talk about change coming into your lives.

In the next chapter, we will take a closer look at the will and the way in the experiences of Mary and Joseph. We will see how well God knows just how to talk to a man and to a woman and what we can learn from it. We will consider the way this good news was introduced to the world. God did not bring His Son into the world through some elaborate coronation but rather through a simple couple, in the lives of a man and woman. The coming of Jesus wasn't first introduced through some presidential speech; rather, the announcement came in the form of a bit of marriage counseling. A closer look at the manner in which God spoke to and dealt with Mary and Joseph reveals much about what He understands about a man and about a woman, things we believe He wants us to know and understand about each other.

Responding to the Note

When I finished reading Pamela's troubling note that day, I could have simply argued and defended myself. A couple of years earlier, I'm quite sure that's exactly what I would have done. After all, I have so many *demands* on me, right? My life is *full.* I'm so *busy.* So many *responsibilities and expectations* on me! You know the drill.

Besides, *Pamela knew I was going into this type of work when she married me*, I reasoned. When I received the note, I could have just rationalized it away. Or I could have attacked her:

What about you?

Remember when you. . . ?

It drives me nuts whenever you. . . !

But none of these "lines" would ever restore anything. I was busted. She had read my mail, and I knew it.

Instead of fighting on, I decided it was time to wise up. So I read the note again, this time slowly and carefully, painful as it was, in order to let the full meaning of it go deep.

Pamela's written · words drove home one point loud and clear: our relationship had entered a danger zone. The question now tensing within my stomach was, *What am I going to do about this?* My will and her way were on a collision course.

As I sat there, thinking and praying, I remembered an old saying: *Desperate times call for desperate measures.*

So I picked up the phone and called Pamela.

"I read the note," I told her.

Silence.

"And I really want to talk about it," I continued.

"I don't want to talk," she said. Which I knew meant she really *did* want to talk, but it wasn't going to be as easy as I might have hoped. She was hurt, deeply so.

I told her I had called a babysitter to watch our kids at home, and I wanted us to go to a quiet restaurant with a salad bar so that I could hear her out, fully. After some coaxing, that's exactly what we did. Out of that three-hour talk, I heard Pamela somehow beyond the words and also began to better understand how she felt. Out of that time we established some practices in our marriage and family life that have been anchor points for us ever since. One, we started Monday family nights—one night a week when we refused to plan anything but spending quality time together as a family talking, having prayer, and having a devotional time of simple Bible study (often highly animated when the kids were younger) along with a fun meal and maybe a game together. And two, we started going on passionate getaways—a few times a year just getting away as a couple to nurture oneness and understanding in our relationship. These decisions are among the best we have ever made, and we would recommend them to any married couple.

At that point in our marriage, Pamela and I knew nothing of the principle of the will and the way, but our marriage was entering a season in which we were about to learn more about it—albeit the hard way. It seemed that just a few years earlier in our relationship all we could think or talk about were the things we had in common. Now the differences we saw and felt in our relationship were almost all we could see.

For us, seven years into marriage, the will of a man and

the way of a woman were at a crossroads. The next turn in our journey was uncertain. This point could have been the beginning of the end. After all, our marriage was broken, but instead of breaking apart, the conflict was doing something different. It was about to break us *open* to a new place of understanding and oneness.

Ask Up!
Questions for Will and Way Conversations

1. What did you think about the method Pamela used to confront Robert at the start of this chapter? What are some other ways she might have responded to the problem or *reacted* to it?

2. Do you identify with Robert's obsessions with work or Pamela's frustrations with how their marriage was "working"? How so?

3. Was the note Pamela wrote to Robert a good, or godly, way to handle the issues they were facing? How so? Would you have approached it differently? In what way?

4. Do you identify with the "magnetic push and pull" of the marital relationship as described in this chapter? Explain.

5. At this early point in the book, do you understand or identify with the principle of the will of a man and the way of a woman? How so?

6. What do you think the apostle Paul meant when he said that marriage is a "profound mystery" (Ephesians 5:32 NIV)?

7. In what way is marriage a metaphor of something of added significance?

Chapter 2
When His *Will* Gets in Her *Way*

Marriages are made in heaven,
but then again. . .so are thunder and lightning.
—Clint Eastwood

From our first date, the only things I (Robert) could recognize in my relationship with Pamela were our similarities. While we came from two different parts of the country—me from the South and Pamela from the North—that seemed to be no major hurdle, at least at first. After all, I reasoned, we had so much in common. For starters, we were both Christians, we both had an interest in working with teenagers, we both liked to go to the beach, we enjoyed music and singing—the list seemed endless.

Maybe my contact lenses were rose-tinted, but for the life of me I could not find any major differences between us. In my mind, we were a perfect match—so drawn to each other and well suited that I could not imagine there would be any real challenges or issues to deal with in our marriage. Pamela was simply beautiful, loving, non-demanding, quick to do things for me, considerate, caring, and a joy to be around. Surely, in my mind, there was nothing about her that would bring any concern.

After we got married, some things changed. So many people warned us about how difficult the early years together would be, but actually they were great. We honestly had so much fun in those first couple of years, just the two of us living together in that little apartment. In a way it felt like playing house. For the most part, you would say we got along pretty well, but we did have our moments. While the fires of sexual intimacy intensified, at times so did the sparks of personal disagreement and arguing.

By the time we had been married a few years, it seemed as if the only things I could recognize were the things we *disagreed* on. *Man*, were we ever different. For instance, we soon realized that while Pamela loved the great outdoors and swimming, I really loved the great indoors and writing. While Pamela loved having long talks and taking long walks, I really loved quiet times, reading, and reflection.

One of the worst days of differences we ever had was on a Labor Day. As I recall, Pamela was pregnant with our first child and at the end of her first trimester. It was an unforgettable day for all the wrong reasons.

Since I had decided to sleep in that morning, Pamela actually got up first and brought me coffee in bed, partly because she couldn't get me out of the bed. By the time she got back up to our bedroom with *both* cups of coffee, I had turned the TV on to a Labor Day telethon. While I was relaxing, Pamela's mind was focused on the workday we had planned for over the last two weeks.

Cease from Your Labor Day

We had just moved into our first home a few months earlier, and there was much yard work to be done. According to Pamela, for a few weeks before the holiday every time she brought up the yard work we needed to do, I would just say, "Oh. Just put it on the list for Labor Day; we're going to get a lot done on that day off." For some reason, however, the priority of those promises had diminished in my mind.

When Pamela came into the bedroom for the third time that morning, I could almost feel her expectations entering the room ahead of her. Something about her tone was off-putting. There was an edge to her first question.

"So what are *your* plans today?"

What I immediately thought was, *My plans today are to have no plans! Doesn't that sound like fun?*

What I told her was, "Oh, I'm just gonna watch a little bit of this show for a while."

Her lack of response was in itself a response. She was unpleased, clearly. But still I was in a cease-from-your-labors chill mode.

For the next half hour or so, I could hear Pamela working around the house downstairs, straightening and cleaning the kitchen and other rooms. But for some reason, each cabinet door she closed was shut a little more firmly than usual, she put the dishes away a little harder, moved the chairs into place a little louder, and then there were—the *sighs*. Every now and then, I would hear her let out another sigh. Each one was a labored breath that felt like an emotional sentence. It went something like this, *"You're. . .being. . .such. . .a. . . lazy. . .jerk. . .today! What. . .is. . .your. . .problem!"*

Every time I heard a sigh, a clang, or a slam, my attention was momentarily seized, but then the chill mode just kept calling me back. The internal battle ensued, but for some reason the chill kept hijacking the will.

I could feel Pamela steadily climbing up a frustration ladder as the morning progressed. By the time the afternoon arrived, I was still relaxing, and she was getting more upset that Labor Day was turning out to be something quite different than what she had expected.

By the time Pamela's frustration registered enough for her to confront me, her sighs had turned to shouts. She had moved from "disappointed" to "seething."

While Pamela had been climbing up an emotional ladder throughout that day, I had been climbing up (or maybe down) a volitional one. As her emotions fired up, my resistance powered up. Not a good combination. While her expectations were being underlined, highlighted, and circled, my ego was being fortified, magnified, and in my mind at least, maybe a bit more sanctified. While she was raising her voice, I was digging in my heels. I think it's called passive-aggressive behavior. So many questions raced through my mind:

Why doesn't she just chill out and enjoy Labor Day with me the way I want to enjoy it?

*Why do we have to get all of this stuff done **today**?*

What's her problem?

Can't it just wait?

I now know that all Pamela wanted that day was for her husband to simply keep the promises he had made about how the day would be spent. But all I could hear were her frustrations and demands. The more intense those got, the more I saw them as an affront to my will. By then, any promises I had made seemed not nearly as important as my will, my self-respect. The more Pamela's expectations powered up, the more my ego did exactly the same thing. It made for one intense afternoon. By the time the argument reached a fever pitch that night, Pamela just walked out the door and down the street of our neighborhood.

She was gone for about forty-five minutes. Later—a good bit later—Pamela told me that as she walked down the street that night, pregnant and upset, she kept telling herself, *Oh, I know he's going to come after me. Surely he's going to come and get me, and he will ask me to come back home.*

But, I'm sorry to say, I didn't. Though the thought did cross my mind, that night my ego had hijacked my better senses. It was a prime example of the will at its worst.

Iron Will

Many women would probably agree with me (Pamela) that men at times possess quite a unique characteristic some might refer to as "stubbornness," "aggressiveness," or even "passive-aggression." Others use a three-letter word: *ego.* Men, however, may prefer to add a dash of testosterone to their description and might prefer to call it "strength" or even simply a "strong will." The events of that Labor Day were difficult for many reasons—none more so than the two very different views we had of them.

There is something about a man exerting his will to plan, to protect, and to provide for his family that, when balanced with a loving spirit, a woman finds absolutely irresistible. . . or in other words, even quite sexy! However, when a man exercises that same "strong will" outside of care and consideration, it stinks of selfishness. It produces resentment and undermines the relationship toward oneness.

The will of a man surrendered to the will of God is a key that helps unlock a successful marriage or builds a successful family. But surrender is essential to honoring God with this strength, and surrender is never easy.

A man's will appropriately communicated and demonstrated is essential to fulfilling his role in a healthy marriage. At its best the man's will provides a sanctuary for his wife to thrive in, a place of support and security where the first is last, where the greatest of all becomes the servant of all, and where he is more concerned about "them" than "him." At that point the atmosphere of the home, the kitchen, and the bedroom changes as God's will becomes the heartbeat of a fulfilling marriage.

God has entrusted man with a unique propensity for possessing a strong *will*. In its proper place, it is a *godly* characteristic. You might ask, "Just how important is the will of a man to growing a successful marriage or to building a successful family?"

The answer: a man's will is immensely important and absolutely essential. The point is not that man is to be some kind of a "god" in his home. *Au contraire.* The scripture calls anyone who proposes to lead his home to position himself as the servant of all. God's desire is to have a solid, faithful, and surrendered will in the midst of every home.

Little did the two of us know on that Labor Day that we were about to learn an important marriage lesson the hard way. While frustrating at first, those "labor pains" eventually helped birth a new understanding in our marriage of a man's will and a woman's way. We began to recognize that while Pamela had a certain "way" she saw that whole day going, my will was set in another direction entirely. The magnetic poles were reversed and pushing hard against each other.

A Different Kind of Labor Day

The emotions and frustrations of that Labor Day meltdown we experienced is something we could have described to you in detail as soon as it happened. However, what we did not know as well then as we do now was just how something so simple could lead to literally ruining a day in our lives. Fortunately, understanding more about the will and the way now has made those dynamics much clearer and easier to spot and confront in ourselves today.

Two thousand years ago, a different kind of "labor" day emerged that uncovers more for us about the will of a man and the way of a woman. In fact, this story not only reveals the way that God was going to save the world, but it also shows much about what He understands about men and women themselves. The story to which we refer is known as the Annunciation, the time when God sent an angel to announce the birth of His Son, Jesus, to Mary and then in turn to Joseph.

These announcements made to Mary and Joseph, were not only the most astounding news any couple ever received, but also ever recorded for us to read about; they reveal much to us regarding the soul of a man and of a woman. In reading the Bible, we are wise to pay attention not only to the words and works of God but also to His ways—not just what He said but *how* He said it. Some of the most helpful and satisfying insights we have ever learned about each other in marriage come right from the story of Mary and Joseph.

Exploring the Mystery

Paul the apostle was intrigued with marriage and its significance. In Ephesians he wrote that marriage is "a profound mystery" (Ephesians 5:32 NIV). In other words, there is more to marriage than meets the eye.

Simply put, when the angel Gabriel announced the coming birth of Jesus to Mary, she was understandably in awe but also quite curious to understand exactly the way this would all occur. Joseph, on the other hand, needed to understand that this was the will of God and that he simply needed to surrender to it. This all becomes quite clear in the Gospel accounts that we will take a closer look at in the next chapter. That "mystery" deserves some investigation.

There are several ways to explore the mystery of marriage, of the union of a man and a woman. As mentioned, Paul invites us to ponder the "profound mystery." Here are some things to consider when you think about this mystery of marriage.

Revelation—Foundational to a Christian's understanding of marriage is what the Bible reveals about it. Some things about marriage are *revealed* through scripture.

Observation—Specialists such as Dr. John Gottman have conducted countless studies on marriage.[7] His research includes following some three hundred couples over a period of twenty-five-plus years. Randomly, his research also reveals the most interesting story about, of all things, the sex life of the porcupine (more about that in chapter 15). Some insights about marriage can be *observed* through science.

Imagination—While the apostle Paul provided some general directives and guidelines for husbands and wives (Ephesians 5:15–33), once again he cited it as "a profound mystery." Some things about marriage wait to be *imagined* through our faith and personal experience.

Many try to turn marriage into a simple *method* with strictly prescribed roles that are often more tied to social expectations and traditions than biblical revelation. Some have tried to reduce Paul's admonitions regarding marriage relationships (Ephesians 5) to a strict set of outdated rules. Without any depth of consideration or imagination, however, they misread and over-interpret his words to men and women to "submit to one another" (v. 21 NIV), to "submit. . .to your own husbands" (v. 22 NIV), and to "love your wives" (v. 25 NIV). While we are tempted to relegate Paul's words about marriage to a rigid *method* to be preached, Paul says they are a *profound mystery* yet to be considered and lived out. Let's consider more of the mystery.

THE GOAL OF MARRIAGE

I (Robert here) have taught many classes on pastoral counseling. One of the questions I always bring to the first lecture is this: "In one word, what is the goal of counseling?" The responses among students usually vary widely and include words such as: *healing, emotional repair, understanding, honesty, forgiveness*, and the list goes on. However, the word we invariably end up agreeing on is this: *wholeness*. The goal of counseling is ultimately helping a wounded, hurting, discouraged, or broken person to experience a greater measure of wholeness in life.

Well, if *wholeness* is the goal of counseling, then *oneness* is the goal of marriage. It was the goal from the start, that "they shall be one flesh" (Genesis 2:24 KJV), and it is confirmed thousands of years later in the Gospels (in Mark 10:8). In fact, Jesus adds a line of firmness to this goal of oneness: "'Therefore what God has joined together, let no one separate'" (Mark 10:9 NIV). In other words, what God brings together as one, no one should ever try to divide. After all, God is the God of unity. Marriage is God's idea, His design, and even His artistic expression. It reveals something of His nature, His heart, and His plan for humankind.

How great it is to see a man and woman growing closer and stronger through the years in their marriage. In fact, one of the most discouraging marriage images we have ever seen is watching some older couples sitting at a restaurant eating their meal, not talking at all and looking at everything and everyone in the room except each other. A hundred times or more we have seen that depressing sight and reminded each other, "We do not want to grow old that way."

The Way at Its Worst and Best

As we found out on that Labor Day years ago, when his will gets in her way, or vice versa, things can get quite messed up in marriage. But when the will and the way learn to move together with grace—that is quite another story. The will of a man and the way of a woman were designed by God to go hand in hand. In the purest sense, where there is a *will*, there is a *way*.

One of the images that helps us picture the will and the way at its the best is that of a dance, even a salsa. (Why not add some spice to this example, right?) For starters, it is so interesting to look online at blogger/dancers writing on the rules of salsa dancing. They actually apply quite well to the principle of the will and the way.

One of the posts was entitled "Connecting with Your Partner—An Introduction to Leading and Following in Salsa Dancing."[8] Does that fit this conversation or what? Here are some of the more apt directions we found. See if they remind you of marriage:

- "Since salsa is a couple dance, there need to be rules in order to move smoothly together with a partner."
- "Leading and following does not just mean the guy says what to do and the girl executes his wishes (sorry guys)."
- "Leading and following is communication and teamwork."
- "We try to split the work it takes, resulting in effortlessly moving together as one unit."
- "To learn how to lead or follow well takes a lot of

sensitivity. You need to be willing to talk and listen to your partner, as opposed to just executing your steps or styling."

- "You can think of leading and following as speaking the same language. You need to adhere to the grammar rules and have a certain vocabulary in order to communicate with your partner."
- "Screaming at each other (forcing a lead) will not make up for clear communication."
- "Not listening (anticipating) will take the joy out of any conversation."
- "Just be sure you learn the language."

We were amazed to see how many of these directions relate to what it takes to have a great relationship as a couple, to have a great marriage, to dance well together in life. Also, woven through them are principles that, when applied, result in a beautiful balance—a balance that is similar to the one that can result from understanding the will and the way and how they best work together. To do so, however, a couple must have a clear understanding of what they do and do not bring to the dance.

Do you see how the *will* and the *way* go hand in hand, in life and in the dance? While arguably in most dances, especially traditional ones, the man (or the will of a man) leads, it is the woman (or the elegant way of a woman) who adds beauty, flow, intrigue, and wonder to the dance itself. This example is not at all meant to imply that men are the only ones who take the first step, or lead out, or initiate in a relationship between a man and a woman—only that there is a beautiful flow that can come from the collaborative connection of the will of a man and the way of a woman.

While a man's will brings direction to the dance, the way of a woman adds beauty and wonder to it. When one tries to dominate rather than collaborate, rigidity sets in and the dance falls apart (more about that in the next chapter). However, when both find a part to play, embrace it, and pour their hearts into it, something beautiful results.

The will and the way in life. The will and the way on the dance floor. The will and the way moving together as one. That's the idea. But it takes understanding, teachability, and practice—lots of practice.

Press on. Read on. Dance on.

Ask Up!
Questions for Will and Way Conversations

1. In your home, what are some of the more common examples of "his will" getting in "her way"?

2. Is managing expectations a challenge in married life? How so?

3. As a woman, how do you tend to manage your expectations in your marriage? What are you learning about yourself?

4. As a man, does your ego sometimes make marriage a challenge? How so? How do you tend to deal with those challenges?

5. What would you say God has revealed to you about marriage? What is clear?

6. What would you say you have observed about marriage in life? How has this affected you and your approach to marriage?

7. Is oneness a good goal for marriage? Is it attainable or unrealistic?

Chapter 3
Something in the Way:
His Struggle and Hers

While your character flaws may have created mild problems for other people, they will create major problems for your spouse and your marriage.
—Timothy Keller

At twelve years old I (Pamela) would often think about that moment that the angel Gabriel appeared to Mary, a teenager. I would wonder, *If God were looking for a "Mary" today, would He consider me?* Was I "good enough" to be chosen as the star player for such a world-changing event? Did I have my act together well enough to be able to handle such a challenging task? Could He trust me? Would I embrace obedience as quickly and fully as teenage Mary, especially in the face of shame or the risk of being rejected? Would I be able to lay aside my own hopes and dreams to fully embrace another plan that I had never considered?

I would love to think I was strong enough, determined enough, obedient enough, but the truth is, just the part of the story with an angel appearing to me in the middle of the day would probably make me pass out! So, I can understand why the Bible states in Luke's Gospel: "Mary was greatly troubled at his words and wondered what kind of greeting this might be" (Luke 1:29 NIV).

One of the beautiful aspects of this story is that God

chose a woman to ignite such a global plan, this plan of salvation for all humankind and for all generations. I would love to think that when God brought His Son into the world, He spoke to the woman first because he knew she would cover the details. In fact, I've heard it said before that if the wise men were as wise as they said they were, they would have brought a woman with them. Then there would have been a covered dish and a box of diapers, and they would have gotten there much sooner! Maybe then they would not have needed to ask for directions to complete the task. (Smile.)

When the angel Gabriel was sent to Mary in Nazareth, he told her that she would have a significant role to play in God's plan. Just listen to this incredible statement he made to her:

> *"Do not be afraid, Mary; you have found favor with God. You will conceive and give birth to a son, and you are to call him Jesus."*
>
> (Luke 1:30–31 NIV)

Mary's response is so fitting and revealed how the way of a woman was deeply at work within her soul and in this moment of history. She did not cry or, like Sarah in the book of Genesis, burst out laughing. She did not run away in fear or pass out like I would have. No, she responded with a simple but womanlike question: "'How will this be,' Mary asked the angel, 'since I am a virgin?'" (Luke 1:34 NIV).

Mary's first concern was to know more about *the way* this phenomenal plan would unfold in her simple life. How true to form when you understand how God has designed a woman. God was obviously aware of the amazing young woman He chose. He knew that ultimately her ways would respect and honor His ways and His will without engaging in a tug-of-war. He knew that her heart would be quick to say, "'I am the Lord's servant. . . May your word to me be fulfilled'" (Luke 1:38 NIV). Which is exactly why God, the great Creator and Divine Designer, chose not only a woman but this particular woman to ignite His plan.

Even more amazing in this story is the painstaking care God takes to answer Mary's important question, "How will this be?" In the next few sentences of the passage the angel patiently tells Mary more about the way in which the incarnation of Christ will take place within the hallowed confines of her womb. Clearly the angel and his communication with the woman models for every man the importance of being sensitive in communicating with a woman and to her deep need to understand the way in which things will be done. Her need for a sense of security is unmet without it.

Interestingly, the angel came to Mary first and revealed the will of God. Immediately she wrestled a bit with some confusion over the way this seemingly impossible thing could be done. The angel explained, and Mary apparently quickly accepted. And instead of hurrying to Joseph and dumping this news on him, Mary "treasured up all these things and pondered them in her heart" (Luke 2:19 NIV).

SHE'S GOT A WAY

The magnetic push and pull of a man's will and a woman's way are legendary. One example was a popular play in seventeenth-century England by a playwright second only to Shakespeare, Ben Jonson. He wrote a play called *The Magnetic Lady* about a woman attracted to Captain Ironside and befriended by two characters, Compass and Needle.

Just consider a woman's way. It is a theme that has filled the world of art. There is something about the way of a woman, something recognized in scripture but also in culture to this day. The way of a woman is so compelling that it even shows up repeatedly in our popular music. Just think of a few of the more popular song titles:

Faith Hill sings, "It's the *way* you love me."
Billy Joel says, "She's got a *way* about her."
The Temptations noted, "The *way* you do the things you do."
Frank Sinatra celebrated, "The *way* you look tonight."
Barbara Streisand sang about "the *way* we were."
The Beatles saw "something in the *way* she moves."
Clint Black sang, "A woman has her *way*."
Peter Frampton said, "Baby, I love your *way*."
Joel also affirmed that he loves her "just the *way* you are."
Nat King Cole spelled L-O-V-E like this: "*L* is for the *way* you look at me."

> At its best, the way of a woman can be. . .
> *insightful,*
> *encouraging,*
> *helpful,*
> and *committed.* . .to a man and a family.

But remember, there is another side to the magnet that repels instead of attracts. While every woman has a God-graced propensity for exhibiting her way and her beauty, she also wrestles with the results of the fall, with selfishness.

There is a compelling or drawing side to the feminine magnet, to a woman's soul. But, just as with the man, there is another side, one that never draws people closer; instead, it pushes them away.

At its worst, the way of a woman can be. . .

> *frustrating,*
> *nagging,*
> *discouraging,*
> *angry,*
> and *manipulative*. . .to a man and a family.

THE JOSEPH CHALLENGE

Once Mary was found to be pregnant, imagine the challenges this news brought to Joseph, and to the will of a man. It must have immediately threatened him on several levels:

> *his dignity,*
> *his pride,*
> *his ego,*
> *his reputation,*
> *his family honor,*
> *his relationship with Mary,*
> and *his plans for the future.*

After discovering the news about Mary, we are told that Joseph had the reputation of "a righteous man" and that he "did not want to disgrace her publicly" (Matthew 1:19 NLT).

While Mary was apparently endeavoring to trust God and her husband's leadership, Joseph devised a plan of his own. The scripture says, "he had in mind to divorce her quietly" (v. 19 NIV).

A familiar picture: a man and his will stuck between a rock and a hard place.

He would get through this.

He would somehow protect the reputation of the woman he loved.

He would come up with a plan.

But what Joseph did not know at first is that God had a plan of His own. He was not about to let the will of a man get in the way of His. So immediately He sent an angel to Joseph to set the record straight. The words God chose to speak reveal how well He understands the man:

> *"Do not be afraid. . . She [Mary] will give birth*
> *to a son, and you are to give him the name Jesus,*
> *because he will save his people from their sins."*
>
> (Matthew 1:20–21 NIV)

How differently God spoke to the man than He did the woman. Did you notice?

"She *will* give birth to a son. . ."

"You *are to give* him the name Jesus. . ."

"He *will* save his people. . ."

She *will*. You *will*. He *will*.

With an eternal purpose in mind, God appeals to the most significant part of a man's soul—the will—and to the most significant part of a woman's soul—the way. He *calls out* Joseph to surrender to His will. He *draws out* Mary to yield to it. God knows that once the will of a man and the way of a woman are ignited together with the noble purposes of God, the world will never be the same.

The same God who made both the man and the woman spoke to the two of them so differently. Notice that altogether He used almost three times as many words communicating this significant message to Mary than He did to Joseph. With the woman, He stated His will, and then He coached her through the way, *explaining patiently* how it would be accomplished. It is as if He knew that this insight would be a comfort to her. With the man, He stated His will, and then He proceeded to *drive it deep* into the man's heart, imparting a purpose and mission to his soul ("you will name him Jesus," Matthew 1:21).

It stands to reason, then, that if in order to get something done God chose to speak in quite a different manner to the man and the woman, we need to learn how to do the same. Let's consider more of the mystery.

THE WILL AT ITS BEST. . .AND WORST

God-given potential, gifts, and graces reside in every man and woman. Yet, while it is valuable to know what a man and his will have to offer, it is also important to catch some of the things with which he innately struggles. At our core, we are all fallen and broken and in great need of God and each other. But the effects of the fall of Adam and Eve are something that men and women, all of them, live and struggle with every day.

Thus, at its best, the will of a man can be. . .

purposeful,
protective,
Christlike,
faithful,
and *an anchor.* . .to a woman and to a family.

That's the upside of the magnet—the pull, the draw.

But there is also another side that pushes people away instead.

Intrinsically, the challenge goes all the way back to Adam and his sin in the garden. Sin and selfishness leave a man empty and looking for ways to fill that emptiness. John Eldredge notes that as men "we are forever frustrated in our ability to conquer life. That's the 'sweat of your brow. . .thorns and thistles' thing."[9]

In fact, at its worst, the will of a man, even on Labor Days, can be. . .

unreasonable,
stubborn,
abusive,
selfish,
unreliable,
and even *unfaithful.* . .to a woman and a family.

Either way, the will of a man is a powerful force, magnetically so.

A man's will can be a tremendous blessing to a woman's heart and to her children, or it can be a powerful curse.

Marriage and Understanding

Staying interested in life, in love, and in each other is the best way to engage the will of a man and the way of a woman. Asking questions. Staying curious. Embracing the mystery of it all. This quest for oneness calls for understanding. The second half of the beloved "Prayer of St. Francis" contains a line that underscores this truth. It reads:

> *O divine Master, grant that I may not so much seek*
> *To be consoled as to console,*
> To be understood as to understand,
> *To be loved as to love;*
> *For it is in giving that we receive;*
> *It is in pardoning that we are pardoned;*
> *It is in dying to self that we are born to eternal life.*

"Grant that I may not so much seek. . .to be understood as to understand." The principle of the will of a man and the way of a woman has helped us to do more of this in our relationship, in our marriage, and even in raising our children. This book presents this principle and some laughable and tearful moments in our relationship that have confirmed it over and over again. Our hope is that as you think about these insights and experiences, they will encourage you to consider, discuss, and even pray about your own.

Did Joseph Have an Ego? Did Mary Question God?

While the Bible does not include volumes of information on Joseph, Mary's husband, it tells us enough. The Gospel of Matthew makes it clear that Joseph was caught in an awkward spot and that, like all men, he had an ego that made it even more difficult. The greatest announcement ever made to a man or a woman was undoubtedly when God revealed His plans to send His Son to earth. But His process of communicating this to a man was entirely different than His way of doing so to a woman. In fact, the manner in which God chose to do so reveals some interesting insights as to what God understands about the makeup of a man and a woman's soul.

Remember, when Mary became pregnant with the Son of God, she did so as a virgin. As startling as the news of this immaculate conception must have been to Mary initially, can you imagine how Joseph took the news? The only description the New Testament gives us as to his reaction was that he, "a just man and unwilling to put her to shame, resolved to divorce her quietly" (Matthew 1:19 ESV).

While Joseph is referred to as "a just man," he was also a man and had a plan of his own for handling this awkward situation once he learned of it. Clearly he wasted no time setting his will in a certain direction. It is so interesting to take a closer look at how God changed his will, at how that process reveals how well God knows just how to confront and shape the will of a man.

But Joseph wasn't alone in revealing some of his own humanness and vulnerability when faced with the challenging aspects of the shape of God's will. After all, Mary, too, must have imagined the future and life of a normal young Hebrew bride-to-be—that is, until God rocked her world with news that would stretch her soul beyond anything she could have imagined.

Mary's first reaction to the angel's announcement that she, a virgin, would be "with child" via this act of God was simply this:

"How. . . ?"

"How will this be. . . ?"

"How will this be, since I am a virgin?" (Luke 1:34 ESV)

Did you notice anything about these reactions or responses from Joseph and Mary? For starters, once they learned of the "interruption" God had planned for their lives, Joseph set his will to put Mary away quietly so that she could save face. And Mary immediately wanted to know more about the way all of this would happen.

There it is, or an introduction to it, at least. Believe us, there are more, many more, beautiful and stirring insights in this story. Many of them can help us grow deeper and stronger in our marriages and families. Some of them help inform us as parents, which we will consider more closely in the next chapter. But for now, these will do.

There is something about the will of a man and the way of a woman.

God knows.

We seek to know more.

Ask Up!
Questions for Will and Way Conversations

1. What does the story of the annunciation teach us about Mary and the way of a woman? In what ways do you understand or relate to this?

2. Which popular song about a woman's "way" is your favorite? What do you like about that one? Are the lyrics realistic and true?

3. How did God's will challenge Mary's ways? And how did she cope with or manage it?

4. What kinds of challenges did Mary's pregnancy create for Joseph? How well did he deal with them? What does this story reveal about the will of a man?

5. What does the way of a woman look like at its best? And at its worst? What other examples do you see in the Bible, in history, or in our current world?

6. What does the will of a man look like at its best? And at its worst? What other examples do you see in the Bible, in history, or in our current world?

7. Was marriage intended to be a "freeing" or a "restrictive" experience? How so?

8. What role does understanding play in marriage?

CHAPTER 4
When Parents Know, Children Grow

If I cannot give my children a perfect mother
I can at least give them more of the one
they've got.

—Ruth Bell Graham

Driving in the car with Kara, our then-five-year-old daughter, turned into an unforgettable moment. As we drove back to our home, I (Robert) was at the wheel, and blond-haired, blue-eyed little Kara Joy was sitting right next to me. But something was different in that moment. She was quiet! And, if there is anything that little girl rarely ever was growing up, it was quiet.

So, I was curious. For a moment, I just wondered what she might be thinking. What had her so quiet? Was she thinking about her friends, her dolls, or her favorite TV program?

Then I simply just had to ask.

"Hey, Kara!"

"What?" Her head turned toward me, her face still apparently lost in thought.

"What are you thinking about right now?"

Without a moment's hesitation, she smiled, turned her head, and said with certainty, "I'm thinking that you're handsome!"

Oh my gosh. Those five words were the last thing I

expected to hear. I felt honored, appreciated, and loved all at the same time.

I have told that story so many times and so often reflected on how surprised I was by those words. In fact, I have re-asked Kara the question time and time again. Over the years whenever I have needed a little "ego boost," I have asked the same question, "Hey, Kara, what are you thinking about right now?" She has always responded with the old answer: "I'm thinking that you're handsome!" Ah. . .isn't fatherhood great!

Even when Kara went off to college, sometimes I would text her to check in and ask the same question, "Hey, Kara, what are you thinking about right now?" I'm sure there were times her first instinct must have been, "I'm thinking you should send me more money!" But she has always kept on message and given me the same response.

A similar moment occurred about five years later. By that time, our son, Rob, was five years old. In much the same way as the earlier story, Rob and I were in the car and driving somewhere. I noticed that Rob was staring at the window and that he had said nothing for the past several minutes. Again, I was curious. What was that little boy thinking?

Now, let me mention that for Rob being quiet at this age and stage of his life was quite normal. He wasn't nearly as talkative as his sisters. Nowhere close. But immediately that moment reminded me of the day I asked Kara a question and of the unforgettable answer she gave me.

So, this time I had to ask the boy.

"Hey, Rob-bo?"

Rob turned his head slowly and looked over at me.

"Huh?" he seemed to grunt more than say.

"What are you thinking about right now, Son?" I asked.

"*Nothing!*" Robbi said.

"Oh, Rob," I insisted. "I know you must be thinking about football, or Batman, or something, right? C'mon. What are you thinking about? Tell me, Buddy!"

"N-O-T-H-I-N-G!" Robbi almost shouted, his brow tightly furrowed, clearly frustrated that I didn't believe him the first time.

Then it hit me. Men have a "mental gear" that women don't possess called *neutral*!

Somehow they are capable of periodically allowing their minds to rest in a somewhat catatonic state and simply shut the world around them right out. This must be why men can sit and channel surf incessantly and be perfectly content to land on one channel and just stay there. Or perhaps this is why they can watch identical episodes of Sports Center back to back on ESPN.

LITTLE BOYS AND LITTLE GIRLS

The oft-quoted, and sometimes misquoted, nineteenth-century nursery rhyme went something like this:

> *What are little boys made of?*
> *Frogs and snails*
> *And puppy-dogs' tails;*
> *That's what little boys are made of.*

And not to be left out . . .

> *What are little girls made of?*
> *Sugar and spice*

And everything nice (or *all things nice*);
That's what little girls are made of.[10]

We both remember hearing this as children so many times. It appears first in a manuscript by Robert Southey (1774–1843). What it meant to us then simply was, after observation, it is clear that boys and girls are different. Many today would like to diminish, blur, or even entirely remove any awareness of these differences. While certainly some of them are socialized and not innate, more nurture than nature, it is clear that boys and girls truly are different by design, both physiologically and emotionally.

Pamela agrees. Also, she tells me that women not only tend to have their minds always running and considering something, but that they even can carry on mental conversations with themselves. She explains it better than me. Take it away, Sweetheart. Baton pass!

I (Pamela here) have now come to realize that "two [really] are better than one" in so many areas of marriage, including parenting. This showed up clearly when dealing with our one and only son, Rob. As child number three, Rob has been surrounded by women for most of his life. He has two older sisters and one younger. The girls always felt like we were deferring to Rob's wants more than theirs, but raising boys is *so* much different than raising girls. The girls, on the other hand, expected a lot of their dad's time and attention. As a result, he treated them like princesses, leaving Rob to "man up." So I endeavored to even the odds for Rob, who sometimes felt outnumbered; he and I had a unique understanding of each other.

I grew up right in the middle of an older brother and a

younger brother; some would refer to it as survival! So, Rob and I could relate. Also, we share similar likes and dislikes related to friendships, understanding people, and enjoying the same types of foods. I also had a unique perspective of Rob compared to my husband's. I believed I better understood why he would cry over certain issues as a little boy. My husband would encourage him to toughen up. I would understand when he didn't want to go to school and deal with the pressures of the classroom, and Robert would try and inspire Rob to have a thicker skin.

One example of the different ways my husband and I parented Rob was in the area of dealing with emotions. For example, every parent has experienced their child waking up in the middle of the night frightened by a dream and crying out for a parent's presence. Robert and I dealt with those moments in opposite ways. Whenever I was the first to awake in those moments (which was more often than my husband), I would go to Rob's bedside, ask him what was wrong, and reassure him that everything was going to be all right. Sometimes he needed me to remind him that God was close, sometimes he just needed me to turn on a night light, and sometimes he just needed a hug. Either way, my role was to listen, understand, and provide comfort for my child's anxious heart.

Robert had a different approach. I noticed that instead of trying to understand our son's fears, Robert often tried to just call him out of them. He would say things such as: "You're not afraid! You don't have anything to worry about! Mom and I are right down the hall! Just go to back to sleep!" Robert acknowledges that often he just wanted to get the anxious moment dealt with so he could get back to sleep. So, while my mother's heart focused on understanding our son, Robert focused more on calling out strength and courage.

These tendencies, we believe, are connected to the will of a man and the way of a woman. While I focused on the *way* he was feeling, Robert was more riveted on the *will* it would require for him to get beyond it. Both of these are important and are needed to help a child grow, develop, and find balance in life.

BACK OFF!

Finally, one day when Rob was about thirteen, we were in a discussion that was getting more heated by the minute. As parents, we were not too thrilled about some of the choices we saw Rob making with his friends. I was trying to handle it so no one would get offended, and my husband was like a bull in a china shop. He wasn't speaking with Rob about the issue; he was barking at him. I was just about ready to confront my husband's communication skills, or lack thereof. I wanted to make sure my son's feelings weren't damaged by this demanding one-way conversation when I definitely sensed the Spirit of God tell me to stop.

"Step back! They are both men, and Rob understands 'man talk' more than you think. Men know how to talk to one another. You could hold your son back from growing into a man if you keep getting in the middle."

I couldn't figure out why the Lord wouldn't want me to make sure my son's feelings weren't damaged. That spiritual prompting was so clear I still remember where I was standing. It was one of those moments. I kept my mouth shut and let them wrestle it out with their words, their wills, their tones, and their aggression. From that time on, I knew Rob really needed his dad. He didn't even know how much. They are two very different natures and personalities, creatives both; but they are also both men displaying the strength of their will. As difficult as it was to admit, they speak a common language that I do not always understand—Man-ese. My conversational comfort zone focuses more on understanding than conquering.

The years ahead of that teenage boy and us were difficult at times, but my husband Robert didn't give up. They struggled in the man cave more than once, but they grew to understand each other. I'm not a perfect mom, or wife for that matter, but I knew enough about the kind of atmosphere I wanted to cultivate at home. I still want a lot of oneness in my marriage, and we want healthy and enjoyable relationships with our once-children, now-adult kids. I sincerely believe the tomorrows I am now experiencing—the joy of watching my kids grow into adults, watching a boy grow into an independent man who will still call his dad on the phone to get Dad's blessing on his choices in life—started in my yesterdays when I heard God tell me to back off and let men be men. He needed his father.

John Gottman notes that a father's impact in a child's life is vital and undeniable. There is a great difference between a father's active presence in the home and a dad going AWOL.

Fathers turn out to be the most critical factor
in the health and success of children across a
wide range of influences. When fathers are not
involved with their kids, there's a five times

greater likelihood that the kids will live in pov-
erty, a three times greater likelihood that they'll
fail in school, and a two times greater likelihood
that they will have emotional and behavioral
problems, use drugs, get involved in crime, or
commit suicide. Men make a difference.[11]

There are just some things that a man best understands about a *boy*.

There are also some things that a woman best knows about a *girl*.

While the Bible provides spiritual and moral direction for parents in how to raise their children, it also encourages us to try and understand them. Curiosity and searching for wisdom is so needed during the parenting years. Understanding helps us to love, lead, and parent better together.

Let's continue the conversation.

Just as husbands and wives are urged by scripture to live with each other "in an understanding way" (1 Peter 3:7 ESV), so parents who understand the principles of the will and the way can be better prepared for effective parenting. For instance, when little boys can't sit still or make eye contact with you, the wise parent knows that it may just be something other than pure disrespect. Whenever little girls are caught playing ballerina when they aren't supposed to be, maybe it is more about development than rudeness. In fact, informed and equipped parents learn to use these differences to their own, and their children's, advantage. Maybe it is more about biology than misbehaving. Little boys with strong wills and little girls with certain ways need time to unwind, to be creative, and to run free.

"I cannot believe that boy is out late again," I (Robert) said to my wife. "Did he not hear the rule we laid down about his curfew? When he gets home, that boy is in big trouble; I mean really big trouble!"

Pamela could feel the frustration in my words and wasn't slow to respond: "But sweetheart, calm down. What do you mean 'big trouble'? What are you planning to do?"

"I am going to give him a piece of my mind," I insisted, "that's what! I'm setting him straight."

"But honey," Pamela fired back, "*how* are you going to say it and *when*, and what *way* are you going to approach this with him? I mean, it is late, you're both going to be tired and—"

I responded before she finished her sentence: "I don't care if he's tired or if I am, that stubbornness has got to be dealt with!"

Did you catch it? If we have had this discussion once, we have had it a hundred times. It is so predictable it could be a script, the same one used over and over again for years, until. . .until we began to see what colored the friction. Did you hear the words? Did you feel the concerns in them? The battle and engagement is one of the will and the way.

The principle of the will and the way also informs our work as parents. One of the most important ways to help raise our children and help them get to the places they need to go is to first understand them and to see where they really are, right now, personally and developmentally. You cannot lead them into tomorrow until you find where they are today.

I (Pamela) have come to realize that as much as our children need the understanding and patience I bring to the table as a mom and a woman, they also really need to hear and feel the strength of their father's will. I need to be careful to remember that. The opposite is true as well.

I (Robert) have come to see that as much as our son and daughters need the direction and support I can bring to them as a dad and a man, they desperately need to experience the understanding and encouragement of their mother's way. We are better together as parents. We share a teaming life. This is an exercise of oneness. But experiencing this involves something we will engage in the next chapter—the practice of *bending*.

Ah, the challenge of the will and the way—but not only the challenge, for the balance of the two is also important and rewarding. Children need both. The fact is, before men's wills and women's ways grow up into hard-to-deal-with *indomitable wills and immovable ways*, they start out smaller and in formation. Shaping a boy's will and a girl's way is a vital part of parenting. Learning how to effectively use intrinsic (internal) and extrinsic (external) motivations in raising our children is vital—a subject we will address further in chapter 10. Understanding the will and the way not only can enrich our marriages, it can also help us better understand, lead, and parent our sons and daughters from the *inside out*.

What Are You Thinking About?

I continued to ask my daughter, Kara, that question right through her college years. You remember, "Hey, Kara—what are you thinking about right now?" Her answer was always the same, "Oh, Dad. I'm thinking that you're handsome."

Then came her wedding day.

Beautifully dressed in white and standing at the entrance to the church with her arm in mine, the music was playing and everyone was in place. We waited for the doors to be opened and soaked in the moment.

"I can't believe it, Kara," I said to my daughter. "Your big day is here!"

"I know," she said. "It is so hard to believe, but here we are."

I had to ask just one more time.

"So, Kara? What are you thinking about right now?"

"Oh, Dad," she said. "I am just so excited."

"But," I paused, "aren't you also thinking that I'm handsome?" All dressed up for the day and smiling, I just had to ask once more.

Her tears flowed. Her moment had come. Her answer had changed.

A new chapter had begun.

Ask Up!
Questions for Will and Way Conversations

1. Do you see the principle of the will of a man and the way of a woman at work in your children's lives? If so, how so? What have you observed so far?

2. Are there some things men and women uniquely bring to parenting? Explain.

3. As Pamela describes in this chapter, are there times a mother needs to "back off" and allow the father to engage or deal with issues their children are facing? Are there times when mothers need to be given room to do the same?

4. Which information and statistics about boys and girls most caught your interest or attention?

5. How does the will of a man and the way of a woman enter into your parenting and your relationships with your children?

6. How can parents shape their children's will without breaking their spirit?

7. How can parents encourage their children's God-given ways? What do children need?

PART II

Bending

Practicing the Will and the Way

CHAPTER 5
Bending Your Will, Finding the Way

*What you have to do and the way you have to
do it is incredibly simple. Whether you are willing to do it, that's another matter.*
—Peter Drucker

Our first big argument happened a few weeks after we got married. We were living in a new place, Rochester, New York, and in our first apartment. As to the subject of the argument, it was so insignificant that I cannot remember much of it at all. But what I (Robert) will never forget is the intensity and the emotion of that first experience. I remember how it made me feel: in a word, *offended*, deeply so.

As things heated up, I remember thinking, *This is bad, really bad. This is getting too loud and too intense. We are letting our feelings get the best of us, or at least Pamela is, I know. We just both need to calm down and count to ten. Time out! Why doesn't she just let it go and chill out? I'm already over it. Why isn't she?*

Then I said it. It just came out of my mouth.

"Oh my gosh, Pamela! This is out of control. If we keep arguing like this, then we're going to end up getting a divorce or something!" I said, urging a temporary peace treaty, or at least trying to negotiate a demilitarized zone.

"Are you kidding?" Pamela shouted. "This is just warming up."

Oh crap! I thought.

"I haven't begun to tell you how I *really* feel," Pamela said.

Man, I thought, *this little girl can really put up a fight. This is getting crazy. My dad and mom never raised their voices like this. At least I don't ever remember them doing so.*

It took us a while, quite a while, to learn how to argue constructively in our marriage, or how to "fight fair" with each other. Honestly, it is still something we work on sometimes. We have definitely improved since those earliest days, but we are also both painfully aware that our default mode is selfishness and the one-sided view that goes along with it.

The way we argue, disagree, or fight (whichever one you choose to call it) has revealed something to us about our backgrounds, something vital to remember. It is this: men and women who get married not only come from two different families, but also from two *different cultures*. In a sense, all marriages are intercultural. Bringing a man and a woman together in marriage is like bringing two different countries together and trying to form one. Imagine saying suddenly to Japan and Iceland, "Okay, now you have just a few days to merge into one nation, one culture, one language, one constitution, and one family."

Lots of luck with that.

One of the reasons we hit such a brick wall in that first big argument was that while Pamela saw the disagreement as a good opportunity to air her true feelings, I saw it as a threat to an already good marriage. But there was something more at work. Not only were a young husband and wife butting heads, but in fact two cultures were starting to collide within our home.

Most people we have counseled over the years have come from one of two different types of home environments when it comes to dealing with conflict. Which type were you raised in—a truth-oriented environment or a grace-oriented environment? While there are certainly varying intensities, in order to explain the difference, here are two types.

A *truth-oriented environment* embraces transparency over avoidance. These are homes in which open, honest, frank, clear, and, at times, passionate confrontations were welcome. Telling it *straight* was more important than telling it *sweet*. As a result, confrontations and disagreements were not at all unusual. But while many things were talked over, it was also considered important to try and really talk them through. Let's call this setting a *truth-oriented environment*.

A *grace-oriented environment* is a home in which open confrontation was avoided at almost all costs. In these homes one is taught to be considerate of others, careful, wise, thoughtful, even (an oft-used Southern term) "nice." Children are urged to "think before you speak." If you had to choose between one or the other in these homes, *kindnes*s was always chosen over *honesty*. Telling it *sweet* was certainly more important than telling it *straight*. As a result, confrontations and disagreements are rare occurrences. Let's call this a *grace-oriented environment*.

Truth-oriented or grace-oriented environment? Which kind of home communication environment were you raised in? Which kind are you now trying to develop yourself?

BENDING

The second relational practice is this: *bending*—continuing to move toward oneness with the person you love involves considering and balancing the differences expressed in the will and the way. This requires some bending of the will and the way in each other's direction.

Generally speaking, men are greatly motivated by the importance of *"Where are we going?"* (i.e., the "will"). They are destination-oriented and often driven to get to that next place. Women are greatly motivated by the importance of *"How are we going to get there?"* (i.e., the "way"). Often in dating and marriage relationships it ends up that *"his will is in my way"* or *"her way keeps contradicting my will."* Learning how to complement each other despite our dynamic and different motivations, or learning how to "bend," is the desired goal. This involves what the Bible calls learning to "defer to one another" or "submit to one another" (Ephesians 5:21).

THE OCEAN OF EMOTION

That first big argument was just like diving into the deep end of the pool for the first time. I have often told Pamela that in the ocean of emotion of life, she is outfitted with deep-sea diving gear, and me—well, I think I only have a snorkel! Pamela just knew how to navigate emotional depths in ways I simply did not. Usually that is a quality of hers that I really appreciate, except for the way she used it in the argument that day.

While things continued to heat up in that first big fight that Pamela and I had as a new couple, the emotions ran high.

In a way, Pamela had her diving gear on and was swimming through those emotional depths. She seemed to be saying, "Wow! It is beautiful down here in the depths! So colorful. So deep. So *honest*. So good. Ahhhhh, let's go deeper!"

At the same time for me, while trying to swim but gasping for air with my snorkel, I was saying, "Oh my gosh! I'm *drowning* in all of this emotion. I can't breathe! It's scary down here in the depths. Time to surface. Quick. I need some air!"

One argument. Two totally different views. In my mind, it was simply *a battle of the wills—mine versus hers*. That's all. Clear and simple.

How would we manage future disagreements and arguments and fights in this relationship, in this marriage?

I wondered. I really wondered.

OFFENSES—THOSE THINGS THAT SO OFTEN GET IN THE WAY
While disagreements and disputes in a marriage may be isolated events or incidents, when left unresolved they could quickly turn into something more relationally hazardous—*offenses*. To feel frustration is one thing; to develop a deep-rooted offense is another thing altogether.

There is a reason that the scripture says, "Do not let the sun go down on your wrath" (Ephesians 4:26 NKJV). Tensions, frustrations, disagreements, anger, and disappointments should be swiftly expressed and processed in a marriage or a relationship leading to marriage. To leave them unresolved is to leave your marriage or your relationship unguarded, unprotected, and at risk.

Jesus felt strongly about this area of offenses and the importance of creating cultures in our homes and communities in which confession and forgiveness flow steadily. Consider this:

> *Then [Jesus] said to the disciples, "It is impossible that no offenses should come, but woe to him through whom they do come! It would be better for him if a millstone were hung around his neck, and he were thrown into the sea, than that he should offend one of these little ones. Take heed to yourselves. If your brother sins against you, rebuke him; and if he repents, forgive him. And if he sins against you seven times in a day, and seven times in a day returns to you, saying, 'I repent,' you shall forgive him."*
>
> (Luke 17:1–4 NKJV)

Clearly Jesus had strong directions and expectations for His followers about the importance of cultivating and maintaining unity in our homes and relationships. In the brief time of just a few sentences, Jesus reminded us that:

- Offenses will undoubtedly come from time to time.
- The initiator of offenses was clearly in His view and at risk.
- If we offend even a "little one" in our midst, we make ourselves an enemy of Christ.
- We need to watch ourselves closely and be quick to forgive.
- When someone offends us, we should confront (i.e., rebuke) him or her.

- When someone repents to us, we should forgive him or her promptly and repeatedly.

The writer/mentor of Proverbs warns us to "above all else, guard your heart, for everything you do flows from it" (Proverbs 4:23 NIV). In reality, the only people who can truly "hurt" us are the ones we care about. And the more we care about them, the more of our hearts we have invited them into and the more vulnerable we become. This is why guarding your heart, and the heart of your marriage, is so essential. We cannot afford to leave any offenses overlooked or unresolved. Be sure of this. Any offense in our lives or marriage left unresolved is most likely growing roots, gaining strength, and going deeper.

Will and way offenses are among the most difficult ones with which men and women struggle. They go deep to the very core of our design. They are the toughest because they not only offend an issue in a husband or wife's life, but more than that, they offend an aspect of their very nature, their internal motivations.

For a woman, the deepest offenses are often those that come whenever *a man **devalues** a woman's ways.* When she doesn't feel she is being heard, really heard, it makes her feel demeaned and uncared for. When her perspective and feelings are belittled, it is deeply frustrating. This leaves a woman feeling resentful and out of sorts. When it happens, offenses take root and, once in place, are not quickly or easily removed.

For a man, the deepest offenses are often those that come whenever *a woman **disregards** a man's will.* When he speaks or shares his wishes or his view on a matter and she quickly says, "I disagree. . ." or "It's not that at all. . ." or "You don't know what you're talking about. . ." a man is frustrated. In his mind, you haven't simply disagreed with his view; you have challenged his will. This leaves a man feeling angry and, at times, out of control.

WHAT MEN AND WOMEN WANT MOST

In order to find more effective ways to communicate with one another as men and women, it is vital that we understand how the will of a man and the way of a woman affects our expectations, our needs, and our desires. Just what is it that women and men want most from one another? Consider this:

What women want the most is. . .
security and partnership
. . .thus they struggle with their expectations.

What men want the most is. . .
respect, honor, and admiration
. . .thus they wrestle with their egos.

ABRAHAM AND JOSEPH

The Bible is replete with examples of God dealing with a man and his will. One we have already considered is Joseph, the husband of Mary. Once he found out that Mary was pregnant, he came up with a plan of his own to deal with it: "Joseph, to whom she was engaged, was a righteous man and did not want to disgrace her publicly, so he decided to break the engagement quietly" (Matthew 1:19 NLT).

Remember, this verse showed us how well God knows how to speak to a man. In the face of Joseph's set will and made-up mind, the angel God sent to speak on His behalf sounded more like a drill sergeant than a cherub:

> *"Don't be afraid. . . She [Mary] will give birth*
> *to a son; and you will name him Jesus [He*
> *Saves], because he will save his people from*
> *their sin."*
>
> (Matthew 1:20–21 GWT)

And, just how did Joseph manage when it came to God's calling him out and speaking so clearly to his will in these matters? Matthew 1 tells us the story:

> *When Joseph woke up, he did what the angel of*
> *the Lord had commanded him and took Mary*
> *home as his wife. But he did not consummate*
> *their marriage until she gave birth to a son.*
> *And he gave him the name Jesus.*
>
> (vv. 24–25 NIV)

In the midst of a tight spot and with so many reasons for his ego to get the best of him, Joseph surrendered to God and chose to serve the best interests of Mary, as well. Just a short while earlier, he was going to "break the engagement quietly," but now watch how his will engaged God's plan:

- Joseph "did what the angel of the Lord had commanded."
- Joseph "took Mary home as his wife."

- Joseph "did not consummate their marriage until she gave birth to a son." (Now, that's some willpower, fellas!)
- Joseph "gave him the name Jesus."

Clearly Joseph surrendered. It shows that God knows how to speak to the will of a man. Just look closer at this verse—"She *will*. . .you *will*. . .because he *will*. . ." He did so with Joseph, but He also did it some two thousand years earlier with someone else: Abraham.

Long before Mary and Joseph parented the promised Son, Abraham was promised a son himself. When he was old and supposedly way beyond his "prime," he was ready to settle with a plan of his own. Similar to what Joseph had planned, it seems Abraham was determined to sort of "help God out." After hearing God renew His promise of a new son via Sarah and with no pharmacy or Viagra around, Abraham said this to God: "'Oh, that Ishmael might live before You'" (Genesis 17:18 NKJV). In other words, *I know you have a promise, but it is physically impossible. So, let's just go with my Plan B.* God's response was as swift and similar to the one Joseph would one day hear:

> But God replied, "No—Sarah, your wife, will
> give birth to a son for you. You will name him
> Isaac, and I will confirm my covenant with him
> and his descendants as an everlasting covenant."
> (Genesis 17:19 NLT)

Did you catch it? Did you see something similar to God's confrontation of Joseph? Check it out one more time:

But God replied, "No—Sarah, your wife, will
give birth to a son for you. You will name him
Isaac, and I will confirm my covenant with him
and his descendants as an everlasting covenant."
(Genesis 17:19 NLT, emphasis added)

When it comes to His plans and promises, God refuses to take no for an answer. Just ask two men: Abraham and Joseph. They found out that when it comes to God and His will, He can bring it to a man in a grace-oriented or a truth-oriented way. Sometimes He leaves that up to us. Sometimes it is dependent on our frame of mind or faith.

God knows how stubborn a man's will and ego can become. It is likely that someone else knows that quite well also—a man's wife and his children.

THERMOSTATS AND THERMOMETERS

There *is* a volitional thermostat deep within a man and his will that is just as real to him as a woman and her ways. Just as she feels the urge to dive boldly into the ocean of emotion and explore its depth and breadth, so he is compelled by matters of the will. This "thermostat" is the soul of a man. At any given time, it can be plugged into *peace* or *anxiety*, *love* or *anger*, *joy* or *frustration*, and *faith* or *fear*, among a host of other drives, motivations, and emotions.

In a sense, it all comes down to what a man will allow himself to live out of. There are a host of motivating influences and forces that can fuel the will of a man. They spring forth from the soul. Jesus clearly placed the responsibility on man to monitor the outflow of his life, to guard his soul, and in essence, to seek to live his life *from* the soul.

Too often, however, we allow our souls to function more like thermometers than thermostats. We *react* instead of *respond* to our wives and our children. There is a marked difference. A thermometer increases and decreases in temperature as frequently as the surrounding conditions change. A thermometer fluctuates with the climate. It is immoderate. It tends to go to extremes. At times, it freezes, and on other occasions, it boils.

A thermostat, however, is quite different. Thermostats instead regulate the temperature of the room; they're not governed by it. Regardless of the surrounding conditions, a well-oiled thermostat maintains a consistent cool when things heat up and a certain warmth when things ice over.

So is the soul of a man who walks in God's Spirit. At its best, a man's soul can sustain him through the worst crises. At its worst, a man's soul can turn winds of dilemma into whirlwinds. His will can easily be hijacked. In God's hands, a soul is a virtual wellspring of heaven. In man's, a harbinger of hell itself.

Consider with me for a moment some of the impulses that motivate our lives as men. This list is best read slowly and honestly. Consider it carefully:

When a man's will *is hijacked by his anger*, he *alienates* the people in his life.

When a man's will *is hijacked by his ambitions*, he *neglects* the people in his life.

When a man's will *is hijacked by his frustrations*, he *hurts* the people in his life.

When a man's will *is hijacked by his fears*, he *overlooks* the people in his life.

When a man's will *is hijacked by his failures*, he *fails* the people in his life.

When a man's will *is hijacked by his greed*, he *undervalues* the people in his life.

When a man's will *is hijacked by his lusts*, he *uses* the people in his life.

When a man's will *is hijacked by his prejudices*, he *offends* the people in his life.

On the other hand:

When a man's will *flows from his soul*, he *blesses* the people in his life.

The challenge and the opportunity in marriage is learning to *express your will* while *respecting her way* all the while. The key practice to this is learning to *respond, not react*.

Your effectiveness as a loving leader is not expressed in how forceful you are but ultimately in how well you collaborate in following God's plans for your shared lives and journey. If both a man and a woman are committed to doing their parts to strengthen the soul of the person they love, it can happen. But make no mistake—there is no magic formula. The marriages that grow best are those where the spouses choose to invest in the relationship every day.

In the next chapter, we will consider some of the challenges women face in navigating a man's will and surrendering their way. But for now, remember just how much a family and a marriage need a man's will focused on and fully surrendered to God.

ASK UP!
Questions for Will and Way Conversations

1. When it comes to disagreements or arguments, do you and your spouse come from similar or different cultures? How does this affect the way you deal with conflict in your marriage and home life?

2. When it comes to the ocean of emotion, who has the deep-sea diving gear and who has the snorkel in your home? How do you know? What are the strengths and the liabilities of these skills?

3. How do you know when it is time for you to bend or yield to your partner in the midst of a disagreement? What informs these steps or practices?

4. How real is the issue of offenses in marriage? What steps and precautions should couples be aware of and utilize in order to keep their marriage as free of offense as possible?

5. What did Abraham and Joseph have in common? What does the way God spoke to these men reveal about what God understands about men and their will?

6. How is a man's soul like a thermometer or thermostat? What does it take to regulate your emotional temperature during a crisis or conflict?

7. As a man, what tends to hijack your will most often? What will it take to resist or overcome this?

CHAPTER 6
My Way or the Highway!

Love has nothing to do with what you are ex-
pecting to get—only with what you are expect-
ing to give—which is everything.
—Katharine Hepburn, *Me: Stories of My Life*

"My thoughts are nothing like your thoughts,"
says the LORD.
    "And my ways are far beyond anything you
could imagine.
    For just as the heavens are higher than the
earth, so my ways are higher than your ways
and my thoughts higher than your thoughts."
—Isaiah 55:8–9 NLT

Life had finally caught up with me (Pamela) nearing the end
of a really busy and overwhelming holiday season. It was the
first week of a new year, and while everyone else was returning to offices and classrooms, I found myself home in bed,
sick. Sometimes when we don't know when to slow down,
our bodies will take control. Little did I know the significance that day would hold for me as I launched into a new
year of hopes, expectations, and responsibilities.

While the house was unusually quiet and I felt too wiped
out to push the vacuum cleaner, I reached for my journal.
As I often do at the start of every New Year, that first week

of January I was revisiting my goals and life mission and looking back over my journal from the year before. I turned on some "mood" music, lit a candle, and enjoyed these unique quiet moments, just me and the Lord. Reflecting on the past year and looking at the new one, I became overwhelmed with some specific dreams in my heart that I was still hoping for; would this be the year?

I've asked that every year it seemed. *Do these things even matter to God?* I wondered. For so long I have thought that these dreams were actually from Him, germinating in my heart and waiting for that moment when they would be realized.

I remembered a moment many years before when I had brought these same dreams and desires to the Lord and He impressed Psalm 16:5–6 (NIV) on my heart:

> LORD, *you alone are my portion and my cup;*
> *you make my lot secure. The boundary lines have*
> *fallen for me in pleasant places; surely I have a*
> *delightful inheritance.*

I realized that the Lord had heard my heart, but for His reasons yet unknown to me, I was to wait patiently and prayerfully as He continued to develop, shape, and transform me. Now years later, here I was still reminding the Lord, still dreaming and hoping. Longing.

In those following moments I entered what has always proved to be dangerous territory. I refer to it as the "why" zone. Questions filled my mind:

Why did others seem to have realized their dreams?
What was wrong with me?
Did I not have the ability of others? Was I inferior to them?

Had I missed a moment of opportunity along the way?

Had God changed His mind?

And for some crazy reason, this all came spilling out of my brain and mouth simultaneously (sometimes it's difficult to tell those two apart):

Am I being disciplined for something, God?

Have I not been the wife you want me to be?

Am I not submissive enough as his wife and Your daughter?

In that split second, I heard my heavenly Father's quick reply through a sudden still voice within. *"Submission isn't your problem. . ."*

He had my attention.

*"Submission isn't your problem, but **surrender** is."*

Boom! That shot right down to the depths of my heart. It seized something in my soul. I felt those words and knew God was up to something deeper than simply fixing my unmet "dream."

Was I endeavoring to please the Lord so I could get something in return?

I cried. And cried. And cried.

He was right, and we both knew it.

HABITS OF THE HIGHER WAY

What is the difference between surrender and submission?

> **Submission (def.):** *to yield oneself to the power or authority of another.*
>
> **Surrender (def.):** *to give up, abandon, or relinquish.*

These two words, though seemingly similar, actually

represent two absolutely different attitudes; to submit is to "give in" to someone else's demands, submitting out of duty and fulfilling a requirement. When we surrender, we "give up" our place and position and relinquish it to another—in this case, putting the focus back on God instead of my own expectations.

Brennan Manning writes:

> *There is an essential difference between submission and surrender. The former is the conscious acceptance of reality. There is a superficial yielding, but tension continues. . . It is halfhearted acceptance. It is described by words such as resignation, compliance, acknowledgement, concession. There remains a feeling of reservation, a tug in the direction of non-acceptance.*
>
> *Surrender, on the other hand, is the moment when my forces of resistance cease to function, when I cannot help but respond to the call of the Spirit. The ability to surrender is a gift of God. However eagerly we may desire it, however diligently we may strive to acquire it, surrender cannot be attained by personal endeavor.[12]*

ADJUST YOUR EXPECTATIONS

Did you know that you cannot have a positive life unless your mind and thoughts are positive? Negative thoughts do not produce a positive relationship, marriage, or life. Negative thoughts spread into our lives, relationships, and home atmosphere, destroying joy like a cancer. Our thoughts can poison a day before it has a chance to begin.

I remember so many days when I would be at home taking care of the daily duties, one of which was doing laundry, and I would find that one pair of underwear still sitting on the floor two inches from the clothes hamper. That would start a one-way conversation that would sound something like this:

How could anyone walk by a pair of his own underwear on the floor?

Does he expect me to pick it up?

He just doesn't appreciate what I do for him all day long while he gets to be around adult human beings.

I would expect that he would realize my life is about more than picking up after him!

Those words would form a mood for the day as they would go around and around in my head, creeping down into my heart and creating negative moments. Also, a huge chasm of resentfulness would grow between us, and the worst part was, more often than not my husband wasn't even aware it was there. I struggled with a growing list of expectations, and soon I realized that it would take a superhero to accomplish them. I needed to gain control of my thought life and renew my mind, but where would I start?

Some women have put together a first aid kit that is often stored in a medicine cabinet, where everything you need for an emergency is neatly packed. Similarly, I discovered I needed a "first thoughts kit," packed with everything I knew I needed to maintain a healthy mind-set (we'll discover the contents later in this chapter).

The "Y" Factor

Have you ever woken up and first thing in the morning you just feel sad? For no apparent reason. The sun is coming up, everyone is getting ready for the day, and even all the underwear is in its proper place! But you still feel this sadness, like a heavy cloak around your shoulders.

One particular morning a similar sense of sadness began to come over me, and I couldn't put my finger on what the cause might be. I sat to have my morning quiet time with the Lord and was distracted by this sadness. I began to consider how many times I had struggled with this unknown sadness, including how much time was being wasted by living within the emotion.

Then the thought hit me: *You can choose not to feel sad.*

What? Is that possible? I wondered. *An emotion can come or go via choice? Really?*

In those moments, the realization that emotions had been driving me instead of me driving my emotions became a transforming awakening itself.

My husband has often repeated the quote by Martin Luther, "You can't keep a bird from flying over your head, but you can prevent it from making a nest in your hair." In other words, I can't keep away all negative emotions and even sometimes the troubling thoughts that seem to come out of nowhere, but I can keep them from controlling my day, my mind, and my speech.

Then immediately I pictured a Y.

Yes, you got that right—just like the letter. But it wasn't a letter per se; it was more like a pathway with a fork in the road, and my mind could choose which direction it would go.

For example, there are those moments we are confronted with the power of a disappointment in something or someone, and that feeling begins to overwhelm our thoughts and attitude. It pours over us, seizing our mind's attention and our mood. It is as though the Y has become a road to travel on, providing a choice of which direction to go. Standing on the stem of the Y facing the upper portion that looks like a V indicates that a decision must be made; the left side represents the emotional journey, and the right side represents taking control, a disciplined journey. I knew if I allowed my thoughts and emotions to travel down the emotional path, the day would become full of negative thoughts.

It is interesting how often we think moving with those negative emotions will bring comfort or bring us to a place of rest for our heavy souls. After all, *I'm just being true to my feelings, right?* I am *just trying to keep it real, correct?*

Often, just the opposite is true. Allowing my mind to be entertained with negative thoughts like *I failed again* or *He doesn't value my opinion* or *Why isn't our marriage like theirs* not only doesn't bring the soul comfort, but it leaves me realizing at the end of the day I don't even like who I am. The emotion has controlled my whole day, hijacked my better senses, kept me from my friendships, and blinded me to what others need.

But the whole time there was another road available, on the right-hand side of the Y. While that side would take more discipline of the heart and mind, I would certainly end up liking who I was at the end of the day, and that was important. Granted, the disciplined path was often the more difficult path, which required endeavoring to conquer unhealthy thinking patterns and discovering ways of escape when life didn't look the way I had hoped. Without the discipline, my thoughts would too often become powerful distractions.

Facing the Y factor and making the right choice is a key to joy in your life, your marriage, and your home. It involves doing something C. S. Lewis described as a characteristic of faith—learning to "tell your emotions where to get off."[13] As we said earlier in the book, emotions are the colors of the soul. They can add much to it, but without the discipline of wisdom and decision-making, they can absolutely undermine your joy, your personal life, and your family life.

Many life lessons have been discovered through what may at face value look like nothing more than a letter Y, but what has really been a journey, a path of discovery, and a place of freedom from myself. In these moments when my faith connects with God's grace, I am not only saved from my sin; I am saved from myself. Choosing my "road less traveled" would call for my mind to be engaged on something that would keep it on a solid track and be renewed. Learning to reflect a Christlike nature through this process immediately began to chase away any negative ideas and thoughts that tried to control me.

Remember, we have the power to choose and decide. Developing a "first thoughts kit" is as helpful to the mind and soul as a "first aid kit" is to the body.

This Y process began to be my chosen path for taking care of aspects of the way I am created. I love deeply. I serve my family out of that deep love. I feel a deep responsibility to those I love, but all of my caring and loving ways need to be managed and governed by God's higher ways, or they spiral down into moments of self-pity that turn me into an unproductive person. The trouble with pity parties is that they never have more than one person show up.

THE CHECKPOINTS

The life lessons I have learned from the Y-factor experiences have remained with me and will always be a part of my personal journey. Honestly, to some extent I think I use this practice almost daily. If you have struggled in a similar way or relate to this way of living, way of thinking, way of managing your emotions or lack thereof, here is the biblical path that I engage in. These are the key insights that become mental "checkpoints" that help draw me away from the downward pull of my emotions and help renew my mind and faith:

> *"The thief comes only to steal and kill and destroy;*
> *I have come that they may have life, and have it to*
> *the full."*
>
> (John 10:10 NIV)

Checkpoint 1: *Remember you have a choice and it is yours and yours alone to make.* Choose life. Our spouse, friends, and other family members can't make the choice for us, but they can surely express their loving and prayerful support.

> *Cast all your anxiety on him because he cares for*
> *you. Be alert and of sober mind. Your enemy the*
> *devil prowls around like a roaring lion looking*
> *for someone to devour. Resist him, standing firm*
> *in the faith.*
>
> (1 Peter 5:7–9 NIV)

*Trust in the LORD with all your heart and lean
not on your own understanding; in all your
ways submit to him, and he will make your
paths straight.*

(Proverbs 3:5–6 NIV)

*For though we live in the world, we do not
wage war as the world does. The weapons we
fight with are not the weapons of the world. On
the contrary, they have divine power to demolish strongholds.*

(2 Corinthians 10:3–4 NIV)

Checkpoint 2: *Make sure you have your "first thoughts kit"
readily available and well packed.* The first thoughts kit represents the powerful insights the Lord has provided for us
in order to find a "way of escape" from the enemy who is
prepared to "kill (our hope), steal (our joy) and destroy (our
ways of loving and living)." When our minds are weary and
full of emotional confusion, it is difficult to have the strength
to fight a battle that appears so much bigger than us, but
there are simple and sensible aids that will begin to assist and
shape a new way of thinking:

> a) Preselect worship music that reminds
> you of God's grace and amazing and higher
> ways. Listen to songs that affirm you are
> loved and rehearse the promises of freedom.
> Worship music is a weapon against negative
> thoughts and beliefs. Remember, King Saul
> would have David play songs of praise on

his harp to drive away demonic oppressions (1 Samuel 16:23).

b) Even in this day of high-tech devices of all types, I've written scriptures on three-by-five cards and still carry them in my purse, put them by my bathroom or kitchen sink—any place I may be still. This leaves little room for my thoughts to wander. Use scriptures that are shorter, strong, and to the point in the version you use. For example, this fits perfectly on a three-by-five and is a great reminder to choose life:

We demolish arguments and every pretension that sets itself up against the knowledge of God, and we take captive every thought to make it obedient to Christ.

(2 Corinthians 10:5 NIV)

c) Use your phone, computer, or tablets wisely. I have learned that in the quiet moments of getting ready for my day, traveling alone in a car, or working out, I can choose what I will fill my mind and heart with. The audio Bible apps (YouVersion, Blue Letter Bible, Bible Gateway, etc.) are lifesavers. Listening to those same scriptures you've written down is reinforcement against negative thinking.

d) Create encouragement texts with your spouse and family text loops. Often Robert and I will come upon a scripture verse and text it to each other, even small phrases. These so often serve to lift our spirits and help us to encourage each other whether we are a few miles away or hundreds of miles away from each other. Also, this is a great way to minister to your children and grandchildren.

Checkpoint 3: *Learn what builds your joy, and be intentional about it.* There are a number of activities that I have come to experience that renew and fill my joy.

a) Starting every day in quiet moments storing up from the Word of God and prayer is an absolute.

b) Being with people. I am a certified MBTI instructor, and one of the most important aspects I have learned from being not just an E, but a high E (for extraversion) is understanding that being with people renews my energy. I've always enjoyed people, but understanding this is the way I have been created has given me direction that has had great payback. So don't ignore what you know about yourself. One pastor and author says, "Know who you are; Accept who you are; and, Be who you are."[14]

c) Being intentional for me is best practiced in the simplest acts. For instance, intentionally speaking words of encouragement to others renews my joy. Engaging in physical exercise clears my head. Planning a trip, whether it is for a week or a simple day trip, provides hope. Making time for fun and creativity, like gardening, my calligraphy work, kayaking, or biking, is like breathing in new air. Your ways may be different. You may enjoy a good book all by yourself, shopping with a group of friends, or organizing a closet. What is most important is that they are *your ways*! Accepting them and understanding them will guide you as you choose life.

When we use the Word of God to not only attack negative thinking but to replace it with His love, His words, and His way of life, we are surrendering our way for a more pure and powerful way, His higher way.

KING DAVID AND THE Y FACTOR

If any Bible character was in touch with his emotions, it was certainly King David. Just consider the emotional heights and depths he journeyed and journaled in the book of Psalms alone. He was passionate, "a man after God's own heart," and a man full of heart. Who would have better learned how to "tell his emotions where to get off" when the moment called for it than David?

One moment when he appeared to do exactly this was in Psalm 103:1–3 (NKJV):

> *Bless the LORD, O my soul: and all that is within*

me, bless His holy name!

Bless the LORD, O my soul, and forget not
all His benefits:

Who forgives all your iniquities, who heals
all your diseases.

In this passage, David seems to be practicing Y-factor-type principles. Whatever he is going through, he takes charge of his focus and reminds his "soul" to "bless the Lord." Notice, he also does this wholeheartedly (i.e., "and all that is within me"). Then, he encourages his heart through remembrance ("forget not all His benefits"). The Y-factor practices, then, can help a woman with her way to stay in check and to guard her heart.

But when a woman is working to keep her spirit and attitude (i.e., her way) in check before God but is still frustrated with the *way* her husband is using or misusing his *will*, what is she to do? More about the right "tool" for that job in the next chapter. Remember, practicing the Y-factor and using your "first thoughts kit" changes the choice from "my way or the highway" to my way or the Higher way.

Ask Up!
Questions for Will and Way Conversations

1. How would you define "emotions"? In simple words, what are they?

2. What role should emotions play in our lives?

3. What would life and marriage be like without emotions?

4. Was Jesus "emotional"? Explain.

5. Sometimes negative emotions can be like scripts that play over and over again in our minds. If you could put it in words, what are one or two scripts that most often try to play in your mind and bring you down emotionally? How do you deal with these times?

6. Do you understand the Y-factor Pamela explains in this chapter? How might it be of help in your life in overcoming negative or controlling emotions?

7. What are some ways that husbands and wives can serve (or minister to) each other's emotional health and strength?

CHAPTER 7
Getting His Attention:
The Ultimate "Power" Tool

As iron sharpens iron, so one person sharpens another.

—Proverbs 27:17 NIV

When Pamela and I moved to Boston several years ago, we had the privilege of leasing a beautiful old New England-y house that belonged to a Congregational church. They were in between pastors for a few years and were willing to rent it out to us. Each year we prayed, and probably crossed our fingers a little, hoping that we would get to rent it yet another year. And for a few years that door continued to open.

But near the end of our fourth year of renting, we came home one afternoon to a message on our answering machine that, in essence, said, "As for you and your house—you need to get ready to move, because we have finally found a pastor." So we had only a handful of weeks to find out what we were going to do.

This unexpected valley of decision came at a most inconvenient time, as such situations often do. First, Pamela had just given birth to our fourth child. Second, my wife's great-grandfather was in poor health, and her mom really needed her to travel out to Michigan more than once to offer her helpful support. Third, we had a child who was having lots of difficulties in school, and these were calling for much extra time and attention. Fourth, I was a busy pastor working in a church.

So, in light of these four points, fifth—let's just say things had really tensed up in our home and marriage. There was a lot to keep our heads around and our eyes on and much that was pushing us forward and sometimes apart from each other. And if that wasn't enough, we now added the big search for a place to live to the list.

All of this combined to create an atmosphere of tension and pressure not only in our home but between Pamela and me in our marriage. We searched the house listings in our area and looked at as many as we could fit in, but we struggled to agree on a suitable place. This led to several disagreements, arguments, and frustrations. I stated my will, repeatedly. She responded that there must be a better way or decision we could make. The more we tried to figure it out, the more, it seemed, my will kept getting in her way and vice versa.

All these changes and challenges added to the tension in our home and the distance growing in our relationship. We found ourselves talking and worrying quite a bit about the living situation and how we would best deal with it. These discussions often led to arguments that pitched up to a level of heat that would lead to nowhere but more frustration and tension.

Even with this big decision of where to move next hovering over our heads, all the other challenges continued: taking care of the kids and paying the bills. To add to this list, we were looking at houses in the area and trying to deal with the sticker shock that hit us repeatedly. It seemed that Pamela and I were at a bit of a loss about what to do and which decision to make. We knew a decision would have to be made within the month, but we also knew she was going to have to be away helping her parents. The stress was rising. She could feel it, and so could I.

Then, something happened—something unexpected.

A BIG DECISION

One afternoon she asked, "Robert, could I talk with you in our bedroom?" Well, any type of proposed "activity" in the bedroom always gets my attention, so I consented.

Well, it was not the kind of activity I might have imagined. Instead, she asked me to come in and sit on the bed with her so we could talk. She said she had something she had thought much about and wanted to say to me.

A part of me probably wondered, "Oh no. Is this going to be like the seven-year letter? Have I hurt her deeply yet again?" This was at about the next seven-year mark of marriage. By this time we had been married about fourteen years. But it wasn't a letter she wanted to discuss this time but a passage of scripture and a decision she had made.

"I have been reading and rereading 1 Corinthians 13, the Love Chapter, lately," Pamela said, sitting on the bed and pulling out her Bible. "You know how that chapter defines love?"

"Yes, of course," I said, having read and preached on it often.

"You know how it says that 'love is patient, love is kind . . . . it is not self-seeking, it is not easily angered, it keeps no record of wrongs. . . . [Love] always protects, always trusts, always hopes, always perseveres,' etc., right?" (1 Corinthians 13:4–8 NIV).

"Sure," I said.

"Well, I feel like God has spoken to my heart through this passage and said something to me about how I am to love you and each of our four children," she continued.

At this point Pamela explained how each of these 1 Corinthians love descriptions helped her see just what each family member may need from her in their lives. For instance, regarding one of our children who was having great struggles in school, she felt that the "love is patient" description was exactly the way God wanted her to show love to this child during this particular season. She told me more about this and referred to several of the descriptions and how each one related to each of our four children.

As I reflect back on this now, I can see how Pamela was prayerfully riveted during this season on not just parenting, but very specifically on the way she was to love each child. She took much time to pray, observe the children's needs, and formulate a strategy she would implement to show love to them in the most practical of ways.

THE WAY TO LOVE HIM

It was powerful to hear Pamela talk about the way this passage of scripture was instructing and guiding her mothering of our children. But that was not all.

"There's more," she said.

"What is it? What did you sense God saying to you?"

Tears began to flow. It was clear that whatever Pamela

was going to say, it was not just on her mind but deeply imbedded in her heart. She struggled to get the words out.

"Love. . . always trusts," she said. Pointing to the page in her Bible, she said, "It says, that 'love. . .always trusts.' Robert, I know we have a big decision to make about a house and I wish I could be here with you to make it. But since I am going to be helping my parents. . .I want you to know. . .that I trust you with this decision. I trust you and know you will decide what you feel is best for the kids and for me."

Wow! I thought. I really appreciated my wife saying this with such sincerity. After we talked and prayed together, I walked out of that room feeling at least a foot or two taller than my already six-foot-two-inch frame. I probably had to duck when I walked out the door not to hit my head.

The affirmation that came from Pamela's words, "I fully trust you with this decision," lingered in my mind for the next hour or so. And then something else hit me: *Oh my gosh, I am going to have to make this decision all by myself.* That's when the affirmation gave way to a little bit of anxiety. First her affirmation made me feel more confident. Then it made me feel more responsible.

Women, remember *the words* you say and *the way* you say them are truly powerful.

MEN AND POWER—THE *EGO*

Power. Our culture is obsessed with it. Our lives are affected by it. Our homes and marriages are vulnerable to it. Just think for a moment of how much power permeates our lives today. Power lunches, power ties, power plays, power moves, power colors, power books, power tools, power psychology, self-em*power*ment. Why, some of us even grew up watching Power Rangers. (Remember them?) Power themes and more fill our homes, offices, businesses, and bookshelves in America. Power is big business, but it can also produce big problems.

Lord Acton famously said, "Power tends to corrupt, and absolute power corrupts absolutely." Would anyone disagree?

Christ confronted a society obsessed with power with something even more powerful than power itself. Love. But a love unlike any we had ever known before. Actually, a new kind of love (Greek—*agape*). A force of love that so powerfully touched and changed the heart of one zealot, the apostle John, that once touched by it, his bio changed from a "Son of Thunder" to "John the Beloved." John eventually wrote about this power:

> *God is love. Whoever lives in love lives in God,*
> *and God in them. . . . There is no fear in love.*
> *But perfect love drives out fear, because fear has*
> *to do with punishment. The one who fears is not*
> *made perfect in love.*
>
> (1 John 4:16, 18–19 NIV)

Power was an essential part of Jesus' earthly ministry. Yet clearly, Jesus displayed His power only when it had a love purpose connected to it.

Tony Campolo writes, "A craving for power interferes with love and destroys personal relationships. The desire to be powerful interferes with the possibility of our being real

Christians. . . . Salvation lies in being surrendered to God, serving others, and giving up all attempts to be powerful."[15]

THE ULTIMATE POWER TOOL

If the scene of the Last Supper had been written according to the disciples' notions, I'm sure it would have looked more like a preparation for war than a prayer gathering. After all, the plot had thickened and the heat was on. The Jewish officials and the Pharisees were moving in for the kill. The disciples' lives were in greater peril than ever before. If they ever needed the power that this revolutionary they had chosen to follow could offer, they needed it now.

What would His strategy be? When would He launch the attack? When would Christ's miracles shift from opening blind eyes to gouging out the Romans'?

What was the power tool Jesus ultimately chose to use? It was a towel. Jesus picked up a towel and a basin of water and made His way around the table, washing feet. Washing Peter's feet, despite his impulsiveness. Washing Thomas's feet, despite his doubts. Washing James's feet, despite his brashness. Even washing Judas's feet, despite his betrayal.

Just when they thought He would take up a sword, Jesus marshaled from the inner recesses of His soul a power more formidable than the world had ever known before. The power of love. The power tool Jesus so freely imparted in that room drilled right through the stony shields covering those men's hearts, and it touched them. It planted something within them that power alone can never plant.

This power is the same love that is available 24-7 to

husbands, wives, sons, and daughters to share with one another. It is the stuff that turns houses into homes, children into mature men and women, and couples into a oneness that reflects the nature and glory of God on earth. And love was not ever meant to be sparingly distributed; rather, it should always be lavished.

Our lives are constantly filled with opportunities and challenges that call upon us to act with power or with love. Power seeks to control. Love seeks to influence. Moment by moment, every man and woman must decide what will motivate their actions, reactions, and responses. Those moments occur when your spouse reminds you that it's your turn to change the diapers, when the kids spill their milk at the dinner table for the third time in one night, when your oldest son has borrowed the tool you desperately need and did not put it back where it belongs. It happens when your authority is questioned, your will is challenged, your way is overlooked, and your plans are interfered with. Power or love. Force or influence. In the home, the choice is master or father, boss or mother. Jesus chose to love *and* to lead. He knew that wielding a weapon could pierce the flesh but that washing feet would open up the soul.[16]

That day in our upstairs bedroom in New England, I am sure Pamela had dealt with several days of worry and thought of the ways she may try to push or insist or demand to just have her own way in the decision we had to make about a new place to live. But she made a very different choice. She followed the biblical directive and decided to "be anxious about nothing" but to "pray about everything" (Philippians 4:6–7). She also chose to lay down her opinion sword and to pick up a towel and basin of encouragement and to make a love move instead of a power play.

"I trust you completely with this decision, Robert."

My wife had heard for years that "a gentle answer turns away wrath, but a harsh word stirs up anger" (Proverbs 15:1 NIV). On that day, she personified the passage and made it real. As it turns out, the way we communicate with each other is so vital (more on this in the next chapter). The results in my heart were absolutely disarming and ultimately empowering.

And oh yes, we did find a house. A timber home, in fact. While it took a little work to turn some of the rough-hewn edges of its design into a place a woman would enjoy, it was only a mile from our church and workplace, a mile from the children's schools, and a place we would live in for the next ten years and build lots of memories together.

You might say it was the house that *trust* built.

Ask Up!
Questions for Will and Way Conversations

1. What are some of the biggest or toughest decisions you have had to make as a couple? How did you deal with them? And what role did a man's will and a woman's way play in your decision-making process?

2. What have you learned so far about the way your spouse desires to be loved or shown love by you?

3. Do you ever find yourself trying to show love to your spouse the way you want to be loved and not the way he or she wants to be? How did that work out for you?

4. Does ego ever get in the way of your marriage relationship and your pursuit of oneness? How so? How do you deal with this?

5. What role does power tend to play in our culture? What are some good ways and bad ways it is used?

6. How does power get used and abused in homes and in marriage?

7. What is the difference between the power of love and the love of power? How did Jesus deal with power in His relationships and in the culture? What lessons could you learn from His example that will help you in your marriage relationship?

CHAPTER 8
The Peacekeeper and the Truth-Teller

Communication is understanding, not determining who is right.

—Gary Smalley

Our favorite question to ask couples frustrated with each other is one that often helps to calm them and their anger for at least a few precious moments. We have seen it work over and again. When meeting with a couple at odds with each other emotionally, you can often feel the ice in the atmosphere when they enter the office. As they take their seats, they look away from each other or possibly fold their arms, showing no effort to move closer to each other. They enter the room carrying a big emotional wall, and they place it right in between themselves.

In an effort to get the couple talking, we have a go-to question that we have used over and over: *Would you tell us about a couple of times in your marriage when things were really good between you and you were close? Describe those times for us.*

Usually the first thing they do is look at each other as if to say, "I don't want to go first; you start. You give the first example." Once one of them gets started, it is always quite amazing. Within moments of reminiscing about better days, you can feel the room start to warm up. The couple looks at each other's eyes as they talk. Sometimes they smile over certain aspects or details of their shared memories.

This warming up in the conversation has even occurred when we have met with couples where there has been marital unfaithfulness. Even amid deep wounds of emotional distrust and hurt, we have watched couples at least start to reengage and talk with each other.

This is the power of remembrance. Closer times, intimate moments, and joyful memories are stored up in the mind. God has designed us in such a way that joyous experiences produce chemical reactions that leave their mark on us.

Jesus knew this, and because of it, He not only taught parables and principles to His followers—He made moments. He created unforgettable experiences often tied to visual settings, artifacts, or stories that caused His followers to practice the power of remembrance.

In fact, the most celebrated moment in the world is the one that Jesus created around a table and over wine and bread—Communion or the Eucharist. This ordained object lesson would become a liturgy or practice of remembrance that would establish a context for remembering what Jesus came for—His death and sacrifice for us. But He did not just tell His followers to "do this," but to "do this in *remembrance* of me." When moments are marked, memories are made.

TWO KINDS OF PEOPLE AND CONVERSATIONS

There are two kinds of people in the world. . .and probably in your home, family, or marriage—peacekeepers and truth-tellers. There is a kind of needle in our soul gauge that tends to tilt more toward one of these than the other. What about you? Do you tend to be more of a peacekeeper or a truth-teller?

Truth-tellers are those individuals who think much about what is right and wrong, good and bad, in line or out of line, success or failure, and on track or off track. When they see their spouse, child, friend, or coworker missing the mark in some way, it is difficult *not to* just speak up and say something. Unfortunately, however, at times they may go too far, exerting their will in awkward ways. For truth-tellers, however, the real issue is that there is something that needs to be confronted.

On the other hand. . .

Peacekeepers are those individuals who think much about what they view as kind and unkind, considerate or inconsiderate, good manners and bad manners, polite and impolite, and oh yes, don't forget nice and not nice (especially if you are from the South, as Robert is). Whenever they hear their spouse, child, friend, or coworker missing the mark in some way, quite different from the truth-teller, it is difficult *to* speak up and say something. This is often because they are more concerned about keeping the peace than confronting the issue. As a result, too often things are left unresolved—things that need confrontation are avoided. For peacekeepers, the issue is often the fear of saying it the wrong way.

Truth be known, how many people do you have in your life right now who are telling you the truth? I mean *really* telling you the truth. Who tells you the truth about you, your weaknesses, your strengths, *and* your struggles? Where do you find candor?

Many women, for example, who find themselves in a

difficult marriage will avoid confronting their husbands. Starved for closeness and intimacy with the man she loves, a woman will often *think* about confronting him. She will probably rehearse doing so in her mind several times and imagine just what he might say in return. A mental preconversation ensues that affects her feelings and expectations. Still many avoid the actual confrontation or just wait until the frustrations peak and it all somehow comes out wrong. Although there is a measure of will within to carry out the confrontation, they question the way it may all turn out. Some wait until it is too late.

Interestingly, one of the key discoveries of marriage specialist Dr. John Gottman, in his research on marriage, is that "expressing anger and disagreement—[or] airing a complaint—though rarely pleasant, [actually] makes the marriage stronger in the long run than suppressing the complaint."[17] Again and again, as he has followed the relationships of literally hundreds of couples over a thirty-plus-year period, he has found that the partner who truly cares must care enough to periodically confront the person he or she loves. Every marriage (and every relationship, for that matter) needs grace and peace; and also, every marriage needs truth.

TELLING EACH OTHER THE TRUTH. . . *AT HOME!*

There are two things no married couple or parent, and no home, can thrive without. You will notice that I did not use the word *survive*, but thrive. The two ingredients that work together to open the hearts of family members to one another are these: *grace* and *truth*. The scripture tells us that when Jesus came to earth, He was full of "grace and truth" (John 1:14 NIV). All of our relationships, including those between men and women, desperately need to be filled with Him and with them.

Few would argue that one absolutely essential ingredient needed in the home is grace. Graciousness, kindness, forgiveness, and "the fruit of the Spirit" (Galatians 5:22–23) in general must color the lives and actions of couples and parents who want more than just a "nice house." Grace is required to cultivate authentic and encouraging relationships and to build a home that is a place of refuge and support.

TELLING THE TRUTH—WHAT ARE WE AFRAID OF?
If the Bible says, "'You will know the truth and the truth will set you free'" (John 8:32 NIV), why do so many of us *avoid* telling each other the truth in our marriages and other relationships? We have observed many people ruin and frustrate their lives and the lives of their spouses—and often their children's lives, for that matter—through this one thing: simply not telling each other the truth.

When we allow ourselves to keep secrets and believe lies, to harbor offenses, life becomes more of an illusion than an experience of reality. Ultimately we create barriers; we hurt ourselves and we hurt the people in our lives. Often, and ironically, the ones we hurt the most are the ones who love us the most.

But why do we often refuse to take the less-traveled road of truthfulness? Here are a few of the reasons we believe that women and men, even parents and children, for that matter, will avoid telling each other the truth:

- We worry about the way it will all come out.
- We're afraid of driving them further away.
- We're afraid of making a bad situation even worse.
- We're afraid of what the truth will look like once it is revealed.
- We're afraid of jeopardizing the relationship.

CONFRONTING EACH OTHER GOD'S WAY

When you have known nothing but peace-maintenance in your relationship, the thought of speaking the truth, the *whole* truth, can be overwhelming. Numerous questions arise:

How should I say it?
When is the best time?
Where should I bring it up?

When spouses confront each other, we need to remember a few things, including:

- Register your complaints without criticizing their character.

Remember, men are wired to desire admiration and will shut down the minute character attacks begin. One way to tell the difference between a *complaint* and a *criticism* is that a statement of complaint or concern usually begins with the word *I*. On the other hand, a criticism more often than not begins with the word *you*.

> Here's a *complaint*: "*I* was so disappointed when
> you canceled our date tonight."

> Here's a *criticism*: "*You* are always breaking *your*
> promises. *You* never do what *you* say *you're*
> going to do."

One method confronts; the other condemns. Men respond much more readily to a complaint than a criticism. When they hear a complaint, they will more likely understand your immediate frustration. When they hear a criticism, it feels like they are in court and you're the judge. It is more threatening than motivating.

Remember, men handle truth best when it is communicated respectfully.

Many women fail to recognize this, and as a result, their confrontations turn into altercations.

Remember, women handle truth best when it is communicated lovingly.

When a man creates an atmosphere of love and reassurance for his wife, he can confront her with much greater results. Too often men confront abruptly. The wise man will remember that he is confronting a woman, not another man. The goal must be more than getting a task accomplished; he should remind himself of the delicateness of her soul, regardless of how confident and strong her personality may be.

In her mind, the *way* he confronts her is everything. I mean everything!

"Speak the truth in love" (Ephesians 4:15 NLT). When the Bible says speak the truth in love, it means speak the truth but all the while *in a loving way*, a loving manner, a loving tone. Learning how to do this and do it effectively is the only way most men will ever be able to deal with conflict effectively.

Ask about asking.

Another way in which men and women can diffuse a lot of tension and guarantee a much more effective confrontation is to ask about asking. Instead of just diving in regardless of the setting and timing, try asking your spouse about his or her preference. It could go something like this:

> "Hon, I have a sensitive topic I need to speak with you about. When would be a good time and where would be a good place to do so?"

This way, you may not guarantee a willing audience, but you do grant them the option of the time and the place.

Give the truth time to work.

Be patient! One big mistake many couples make when they confront each other is *pushing* the truth instead of *presenting* it. When a spouse does not get the immediate reaction he or she was hoping for (i.e., regret, remorse, apology, etc.), the tendency is to ball up the truth and repeat it until the spouse gets the emotional reaction he or she wants. Guess what? It will never come that way. And besides, the Bible says, "The wrath of man does not produce the righteousness of God" (James 1:20 NIV).

This calls for trusting in the power of truth to do its own work. Our responsibility is to effectively communicate it. If we are on target, it is God's responsibility to turn it into conviction and, eventually, into change.

Stay on the issue—don't sidetrack, stonewall, or backload.

In an effort to emphasize our point or add weight to our "case," we are often tempted when confronting to get off track. Instead of staying on the specific issue or problem we are dealing with, it is easy to jump into other areas of complaint and criticism. When we do this, we dilute the issue we began with and dig ourselves into a hole. Stay focused when you're confronting. Remember, "Love. . .keeps no record of wrongs" (1 Corinthians 13:4–5 NIV).

MARRIAGE AND EXPECTATIONS

Every now and then I (Robert) like to ask students a relationship question. Usually it goes something like this: *You know that person that you really are interested in, or in love or like with right now? And do you know the things that you really like about them and your relationship with them? Well, when you get married, those things are going to be a hundred times better. Why? Because you will be sharing life then 24-7.* Often that statement is met with smiles. Then, I like to add this into the mix: *You know the things that you really **don't** like about that person and your relationship with them? Well. I'm just saying. . .*

One of the greatest influences on your marriage is the way you *think* about your marriage. Your thoughts about marriage, and in particular the *way* you think about *your* marriage, is vital to how strong or weak it is, even today. Let us explain.

For one, it comes down to expectations. Expectations are powerful motivators in marriage. In some ways expectations can lift a marriage to great heights. After all, our beliefs have an impact on our expectations. For example, in sports it is doubtful that you will be able to win a game if you don't have some expectation that you can do so. Expectation and hope are quite similar. And every marriage needs hope. We need to be able to believe that something extraordinary can happen, something good.

However, unrealistic or uninformed expectations can also be a powerful drain on your marriage. For instance, if your expectations are exaggerated or unrealistic, then you set yourself up for discouragement, perhaps a lot of it. If hopeful expectations fully discount issues of truth, false hopes can form in our minds. This can lead to great frustration.

When your expectations are a mile high and your reality is only a quarter-mile high, what is the difference between them? In other words, from the top of your realities to the bottom of your expectations, what exists in that space? In a word, it is S-T-R-E-S-S.

Yes, when your expectations are higher than your

realities, *stress* is created. It is the result. It exists in that space. Could it be that the stress you feel in your relationship with your spouse or fiancée or boyfriend/girlfriend right now is mostly of your own making?

Before you get upset and put the book down, hold on a moment. Consider just a bit more.

So, in light of this "hope principle," the only way to reduce the stress in your marriage is to do one of two things, or a bit of both. They are:

> 1) To lower your *expectations*, or
> 2) To change (or raise) your *realities*, or
> 3) To adjust both of these somewhat.

This type of stress is actually chronic in that we carry it around with us on the front of our minds. For example, if you expect your spouse to act like someone with five years of marriage experience when you've only been married one year, you are setting yourself up for disappointment and one sick heart.

This principle also works in marriage, dating, and any relationship between men and women. In fact, in his epistle Peter instructs husbands "[to] live with [their] wives in an understanding way, showing honor to the woman" (1 Peter 3:7 ESV).

When we nurture unrealistic expectations, we fuel more and more stress in our minds and souls, and in our relationship. So every day we have a choice to make: either let stress build up through unrealistic expectations or disarm the stress by finding a way to reduce our expectations and take a more honest, informed, and realistic view.

Practice Honor in Your Marriage

Have you ever found yourself in a circle of honor? I (Robert) did for just a few minutes many years ago. They were life-transforming minutes, and I will never be the same.

Barely seventeen years old and newly converted to Christ, I was in the foyer of my downtown home church wearing a robe and making my way toward the baptistery when it happened. My sixty-eight-year-old pastor, standing in line next to my unsuspecting parents and me, enthusiastically asked a visiting guest speaker, "Have you met this young man? Well, let me introduce you to him. This is Robert Crosby." *Is he talking about me?* I wondered. "God is doing great things in this young man's life, and we are excited about his future!"

Although my pastor had ministerial duties to perform that night, such as baptizing a bunch of new believers, hosting a guest evangelist, and leading the congregation— and no more than a few moments to spare—the words he chose filled something within me. At once I felt affirmed, appreciated, and significant. I felt honored.

One of the worst mistakes a husband, wife, father, or mother can make is to allow his or her family to feel undervalued. A key part of a spouse's or parent's role is to remind the ones they love of how valuable and important they are to them, to one another, and most of all, to God Himself.

A lack of honor from a spouse or parent demotivates and discourages the soul. There are perhaps few things more frustrating than being in a family whose members do not affirm and appreciate one another consistently.

When we honor each other boldly and openly,

even in front of others, we do something glorious and unforgettable. In fact, we reflect the practices of the members of the Trinity who constantly honor each other (see, John 5:19, 14:15–31; Matthew 3:17).

Not only are we living today in a culture that is losing its way in affirming and honoring people, but it has at the same time become more adept at sarcasm, dishonor, and criticism. In such a world, circles of honor stand out and "shine as lights in the world" (Philippians 2:15 ESV). Draw those "circles" every day in your marriage and home.

CARVING OUT AN HONEST RELATIONSHIP

Dr. Henry Cloud, noted relationship expert, has written much on how to detect "safe" people. He has written, "This is one of the marks of a truly safe person: they are confrontable."[18]

As long as there are buried resentments, hidden doubts, concealed frustrations, and covered-up wounds, there is no hope whatsoever for real intimacy in a marriage or parenting relationship. Choosing to be a truth-teller is a daring step. Learning to listen deeply is another one (more about this in the next chapter). There is no way to be truly knit together in soul with the person you love without learning how to tell him or her the truth.

Only truth can make way for grace. Think about it. Before you received the *grace* of God's forgiveness, you had to acknowledge the *truth* that you were a sinner, lost and without God. Acknowledging this truth created a hunger for the much-needed grace God has to offer. In like manner, the only way we can experience the grace God wants to impart within our relationships is to acknowledge the truth about them. Truth makes way for grace.

Lastly, if you are in a relationship where trying to tell the truth has brought even more rejection, perhaps even abuse, then you need to find a godly counselor and soon (a pastor would be helpful). However, for most, the answer is simply a prayerful determination to speak the truth, to speak it in love, but to speak it nonetheless.

Ask Up!
Questions for Will and Way Conversations

1. What is a great question that couples need to ask themselves periodically to help them grow in their marriage relationship?

2. Peace-keeper or truth-teller—which do you tend to be in your marriage and relationships? How can you tell?

3. In what ways does fear keep us from telling the truth to each other? How can we overcome this?

4. What is important to keep in mind when confronting a man? What have you learned?

5. What is important to keep in mind when confronting a woman? What have you learned so far?

6. How do expectations in marriage affect your relationship? What are some areas in which you need to adjust your expectations of your spouse or of yourself?

7. What does it mean to "speak the truth in love" (Ephesians 4:15 NLT)? How should that look in a marriage?

CHAPTER 9
Attunement:
Listening with Your Third Ear

Being heard is so close to being loved that
for the average person, they are almost
indistinguishable.

—David Augsburger

Before writing the note we focused on in chapter 1, I (Pamela) spent a lot of time in thought and prayer. I probably wrote it in my mind a hundred times before putting it into an envelope and taping it to the door. I had tried to communicate my hurts earlier in so many different ways, but due to either the tone of my voice (which he sometimes labeled as "whiny"), my explosive words (sprinkled with anger), or the time of day he came home (bad timing), I was at a loss.

A quote from one leader's wife that I will never forget said, "Study your man like the rare beast that he is!" The speaker continued to encourage women to study their man's habits, his likes and dislikes, his strengths and weaknesses, moods and mannerisms. I took that to heart and began to take some mental notes. Bottom line, a fulfilling marriage takes understanding each other. . .sometimes *a lot* of understanding. To study your partner's ways, opinions, joys, and disappointments is to understand him or her, and with that, to better know how to make this thing called marriage work. So I tried to understand what ignited his will to come my way.

First, I noticed that at the end of a long day of dealing with people, leading and resolving many staff and team conflicts, he did not want to come home and deal with more. At first I thought his number one priority was to listen to me, to hear what my concerns of the day were, to be my sounding board. My expectations told me, "If someone *really* loved me, that is what he would want to do to show me how much he genuinely loved me." Instead, Robert looked forward to coming home to a family who was looking forward to seeing him...with enthusiasm! So I noticed that he would often get that glazed look over his face when I began to go over my list of frustrations and disappointments.

I also noticed that when we hit the point of no return in disagreements that led to the all-out watch-your-mouth arguments, it felt quite cathartic for me, but it had an opposite reaction for him. For me it was like a pressure valve that was releasing all the built-up resentment I held on to, and admittedly it felt great to let go! Robert might refer to it more as a session of spewing out resentments and disappointments, and I noticed it made him feel anything but great. In the face of anger he would inwardly withdraw from me and move into his unseen mental man cave. His eyes would sort of roll back in his head, and I couldn't reach him. This only added steam to my experience.

How can I get him to not just listen but really hear me? Those wise words kept returning to me and I began to take them to heart—"study your man." So I started to pay closer attention to what caught his attention, and I noticed he would quote almost everything he read. He studied profusely all the time, whether he was preparing a sermon or an article or just to gain more information. He would often begin sentences this way: "This is what I learned the other day from an author I really respect. . ." "I'm really enjoying this new book I'm into, and this quote has changed my perspective. . ." All of a sudden, *ding-ding-ding*! The alarm went off, and I realized he "hears" what he reads! He takes it to heart and allows it to roll over in his brain, and I watched the information affect his lifestyle. Eureka! In the College of Communicating with Robert, I was on to something.

Now, influence comes in all kinds of forms, but it's all about how you use the information you have. I saw this as a useful tool to get my point across in a way that would potentially eliminate the issues that blocked our communication. That's when I decided I would wrap my wake-up call to Robert in a much-prayed-over-and-thought-about card in order to get the information to him peacefully in a language form he prefers.

Change It Up—The Way You Confront

Jessie Potter wisely said, "If you keep doing what you've always done, you're going to keep getting what you have always gotten."[19] That principle holds true in so many aspects of life, but in none more so than communication and confrontation in marriage.

When I (Robert) think back to that now-infamous seven-year-mark letter, one thing is so clear to me: When Pamela wrote that letter, she had "read" me so well. Not only by that time had she lived with much growing frustration, but she had clearly prayed, sought wisdom, and applied herself to understanding the best way to communicate her challenges to me so that I could hear them at a deeper level—in a way that would disarm my knee-jerk defenses and open me up to hearing more than her voice, but also her heart. Pamela modified, or *attuned*, her approach, and something changed as a result.

By now, it is clear to you that one of the most challenging, and needed, disciplines for me to learn in our marriage has been to listen well, to really hear what Pamela has to say. The longer we are married, the more I find that she needs me to do more than "listen" functionally and physiologically, but also to listen emotionally. While for me, I have often thought that if I am simply present physically and hear her concerns audibly, that will be enough. But she needs more than that.

This is where understanding the will of a man and the way of a woman is invaluable. When a woman wants to confront a man, it is vital that she remembers this: *men handle truth best when it is communicated in a certain way—respectfully and honorably.* Many women fail to recognize this, and as a result, their well-meaning confrontations turn into conflicted altercations. In those cases, men cannot hear the topic because the tone is too much in the way. But you see, when Pamela decided to move her communication from criticism to sincere concern, something changed. I began to hear her at a deeper level.

The Art of Attunement

When it comes to navigating that ocean of emotion we discussed earlier, I still have not become a certified master diver—not by a long shot. In fact, I still find my sinful default mode drives me back again and again to putting my own interests before Pamela's and other people's. Overcoming this tendency is a daily struggle, but I see that enemy more clearly now for who he is.

One of the best strategies for learning to listen well in our marriage has come from Dr. John Gottman. He refers to the practice as *attunement*. The process is not rocket science, but its impact is powerful. Just as it takes a few regular adjustments to tune your favorite radio station in while on a car ride, listening well involves more than just *not* talking. There is a focusing or tuning of self that is required to engage the type of listening a wife really needs from her husband.

"He doesn't listen to me." That is not only one of the most common complaints Pamela has had over the years in our marriage but also one that we hear about often from other couples.

For most women, meaningful conversation is so important that they not only know how to converse with other people, but they have the capacity to carry on mental conversations in their minds even when they are alone. There is a great need for conversational engagements that are authentic and meaningful.

Gottman further describes the process this way:

> *When men "attune" to their women, there is less fighting, more frequent (and better) sex, and both men and women no longer feel so alone. It*

is also the skill that leads to genuine emotional connection, which in turn leads to trust, which in turns leads to you giving women the number one thing they need and want. In other words, this is a big deal. . . . In essence, attunement is learning how to hear and not react, but rather to understand, empathize and supportively respond. It comes when you choose instead of challenging a woman's feelings as "not based on a fact," to instead recognize that in a real sense for her the feeling is a "fact."[20]

Attunement requires some focus and attention. No, it doesn't mean that she is always right, but it does mean that you make a decision that—more important than dueling over who is right—it is more important that you are living in right relationship with each other. Your goal is oneness. Attuning is a skill and requires practice. However, the more you practice it, the better you become. The key is to keep practicing. You can start practicing this today. Here are the steps to follow Gottman's strategy:

A-TT-U-N-E—LISTENING WITH YOUR THIRD EAR

(A) *Attend* to the needs of your wife. When you provide focused attention to your wife, it also feels like affection. Remember, to her attention *is* affection.

(TT) *Turn toward* your wife. Women desire face-to-face interactions. Men, on the other hand, tend to focus more on side-by-side relationships, such as playing golf or going fishing together with a friend. The result of such cultural grooming is that most men do not have a close male friend. Men struggle to break beyond having mere acquaintances, beyond only competing as buddies on a battlefield or golf course.

In her book *The Friendships of Women*, Dee Brestin sizes up the situation quite well:

> *Studies indicate that men, like boys, do things together—rotary, softball, hunting—but they do not often relate to each other as confidants. Men tend to be side by side, engrossed in an activity, whereas women will be face to face. Men may confuse quantity of time spent in the company of other men with intimacy. . . Most men not only find it difficult to make themselves vulnerable to each other, but they are often uncomfortable being together unless their attention can be centered on activity.[21]*

I will never forget the scene. It was the last week of the school year, and Pamela and I were visiting a Christian elementary school that we were considering for our children. Taking a walking tour with the principal through each class, she warned us things might be a bit off routine and relaxed.

When we arrived at the third-grade class, we noticed that the desks were arranged a bit unusually. The teacher explained, "Please excuse us. I told the kids that they could set up their desks any way they desired, and this is the way they chose."

Scanning the arrangement, a light bulb went off over my wife's head and mine. Interestingly enough, the desks were distinctly separated into two groups—boys and girls.

No surprise, right? Well, what was most interesting was that all the guys had lined their desks up, you guessed it, side by side, one right alongside another. And the girls? Face to face and two by two. Pamela, who had just begun reading Brestin's book, picked up on it right away. Even these third-graders exhibited the different manner in which males and females forge friendships—side-by-side and face-to-face, respectively.

So, husband, listening the way your wife needs you to listen is going to be something different than just another few minutes of golf. She needs you to *turn toward* her physically and emotionally.

(U) *Understand*—It is important to ask questions about how or what she is feeling. Remember, as the "Prayer of St. Francis" says, to seek to "understand," not just be "understood." That will require some time and consideration of not only what she thinks but thinking more about how she must feel. This kind of attention is almost irresistible to her. While you may think of it merely as "extra effort" or "work" to listen so hard, she feels it as love, true love.

(N) *Nondefensively listen*—Remember to respond, not react, to what you hear. Even if she is upset, hear her clearly and hear her through. Listen and respond. If her words tap a frustration or negative emotion in you, don't let it coopt your equilibrium. Breathe and calm yourself down if you feel the urge to react or overreact to what you hear.

Gary Smalley says, "If a man truly wants to communicate with his wife, he must enter her world of emotion."[22]

(E) *Empathize*—When you listen long enough that what you hear from your wife goes beyond a simple auditory processing and turns into an emotional understanding, then your third ear is fully engaged. That's what she is looking for from you and sometimes desperately needs. You become the person who will listen to her as will no one else. Her friend and her spouse in those moments becomes her soulmate.

Gottman says, "Neurologists have found that the emotional part of the brain calms down as soon as it feels connected to another person and not alone."[23] Remember, the most important thing in these moments is not who is right or who is wrong, but more so about the two of you being in oneness as a couple.

A-TT-U-N-E is such a great tool that we recommend memorizing it and using it often. Tuning in to each other's concerns and needs is when marriage is more than just a certificate or agreement; it is a practice and a lifestyle. It is one of the ways "these two shall become one."

THE WONDERS

One executive coach, Ed Batista, recently noted that a problem for married couples is that when they get home from work, they often get into arguments within the first fifteen minutes. He says that whenever the first few minutes at home together go well, "it can help both parties feel a sense of care and appreciation that helps them unwind and feel better prepared for the following day."[24] But on the other hand, when it goes badly, it can "poison the rest of the evening."

A pastor I worked with a few years ago admitted that he really was finding he and his wife getting into arguments often within the first few minutes after getting home. Finally he recognized that one of the problems was that he was arriving home each day in a much too self-consumed frame of mind. The "king" arrived home at his "castle" hoping the "queen" would be waiting to help him unwind from another "difficult and long day." The problem was, she often felt the same way. So, he came up with a plan.

"I had to find a marker on my way home from work, a landmark that would remind me to stop thinking about me and my day and to start thinking about my wife and what kind of day she might have had," the pastor said. After hearing his approach, I could relate. I realized I was too often doing the same thing. So, I came up with a marker point of my own and a set of questions that I have come to refer to as "the Wonders." Here they are:

"I *wonder* what kind of day Pamela has had today."

"I *wonder* what kind of mood she will be in when I get home."

"I *wonder* what her greatest joy has been today."

"I *wonder* what her biggest frustration has been today."

"I *wonder* what I could do or say in the first five minutes after I get home to help her feel loved and glad to be home with me."

"I *wonder* what game will be on television when I get home." (*Oops, how did that one sneak in there? Disregard!*)

IT'S ABOUT FEELING, NOT FIXING
One of the most important things for a man to remember in the practice of attunement with a woman is that the goal

is not finding and fixing whatever is bothering her. No, it is more about trying to feel just a bit of what she is feeling. And to do so, you have to listen for a while. To catch the passion she feels over her concern, you have to gain a bit of the perspective she has.

This was confirmed by a recent study done by Harvard Medical School[25] that found wives or girlfriends were generally pleased whenever their spouse or partner showed any emotion. In their minds, this demonstrated that their relationship was healthy. Actually, whenever the women reported that the man realized they were angry, upset, or unhappy, the women reported being happier themselves, even though the men in the same study were not. Much the same way that the Bible urges us to "rejoice with those who rejoice, weep with those who weep" (Romans 12:15 ESV), so it appears a wise man will learn to do the same.

Dr. Shiri Cohen, the researcher of this study, said:

> *It could be that for women, seeing that their male partner is upset reflects some degree of the man's investment and emotional engagement in the relationship, even during difficult times. This is consistent with what is known about the dissatisfaction women often experience when their male partner becomes emotionally withdrawn and disengaged in response to conflict.[26]*

Interestingly, the findings also suggested that men are more satisfied in their marriages when they can read their spouse's positive emotions. On the contrary, women were more satisfied when they perceived their partners were trying to understand their negative emotions. The man's accuracy at discernment was not a key factor; his simple efforts and attempts were.

LOOKING THROUGH THEIR LENS

It is amazing how "right" and "justified" I am when I am looking through my own lens. Often in marital and premarital counseling, I will remove my reading glasses from my pocket and hand them to the man or the woman. Usually I follow it with a request like this: "Describe for me how this issue in your marriage must look through your spouse's (or fiancé/e's) lens. What must it look like to them? How would they describe it?"

This immediately stretches the counselee to look beyond his or her own self-tainted view of the problem and to consider another view, that of his or her spouse. This is a great way to practice what the apostle Paul taught when he wrote that we should put the interests of others before our own interests (Philippians 2:4). In fact, to take it a step further, we would suggest you ask God to give you "grace-tinted" lenses through which to view your spouse.

When you wear grace-tinted lenses, you will grow even more in understanding each other. This applies to parenting as well (more on this in the next chapter). And grace-tinted glasses help you see three things that are vital to bringing a blend into your marriage (something we will look at in the last part of this book). When grace gets in your view, you can see that:

Your spouse is who he or she is today *by the grace of God*.

You are who you are today *by the grace of God*.

You accept your spouse as he or she is today *by the grace of God*.

Now, remember, grace is not something in relationships that we use as a trump card to minimize our own mistakes. We should not go to our spouse and say, "Well, you have to forgive me because if you don't you are not showing grace." No, what we are talking about is you being responsible for your own actions and contributions to your marriage and relationship; not only being in tune, but attuned to each other.

Ask Up!
Questions for Will and Way Conversations

1. What do you think about the statement at the beginning of the chapter: "Study your man like the rare beast that he is"? What are you learning about communicating with your spouse?

2. What is it that sometimes works against us communicating with respect and honor when we talk to each other in marriage or in our relationships with the opposite sex?

3. Are there any changes you need to make to the way you confront tough issues or conflicts with your spouse? What steps will you take to do so?

4. How important is practicing *attunement* to a woman? Do you relate to this need in your relationship?

5. What is an "I wonder" question you could ask on your way home each day that would help you tune in better to your spouse and his or her needs?

6. What is it about men that so often makes them want to try and "fix" their wife's problem instead of hearing them out fully and connecting to them emotionally? Can you relate?

7. If you were to look at your marriage right now through your spouse's lens, what would you see? What is going well? What is not?

CHAPTER 10
A Parent's Path:
The Best Way to Lead Will

A good question can open a conversation; a great one can open a soul.

Elevators reveal a lot about children, especially little ones. It shows up on elevators anywhere. Surely you have experienced it. You know the feeling.

Adults file onto a busy elevator, suddenly silencing whatever conversation they were having or whichever tune they might have been humming or listening to en route. We enter the chamber and dutifully take our places. We all know the unwritten rules of elevator riding, don't we?

Rule number one—*do not look at anyone else while on the elevator*. Eye contact is strictly forbidden. If you must look somewhere, there are only a few places that are permissible, including the changing floor numbers illuminated above the door, the door itself, your wristwatch, your cell phone, or if you must, your shoes. But whatever you do, don't dare look another person in the eye. That's a capital crime.

Rule number two—*everyone must face the door*. Without exception, elevator passengers must stand parallel to the door. If there are two doors, you face the one that just closed, or. . .is it the other one? The slightest degree change in angle or position could disrupt the whole system of order.

Rule number three—*elevator rides must only be endured, never enjoyed.* If you are smiling, laughing, or having any fun whatsoever beforehand, then that must cease once you enter *the chamber.* Don't ask why, that's just how it works.

Rule number four—*absolutely no talking with other passengers.* Everyone aboard must maintain a constant vigil of silence. Not only is talking taboo, but all noises must be avoided, including sneezing, coughing, laughing, humming, etc.

Rule number five—*do not breathe, at least not so that anyone can hear you.* Keep your lungs in a state of suspended animation.

Rule number six—*do not get any closer than you must to the other passengers.* The standing rule is to keep as much space between you and them as possible. For example, if there are only two of you aboard, the appropriate place to stand is at opposite corners, kind of like prizefighters just prior to a round. This is especially true in hospital elevators, where people may be carrying infectious diseases or germs.

These are the unwritten rules of elevator riding. We all know them, right?

Elevators rides tell us a lot about ourselves. What a picture. Only a brief journey and yet a cabled cube full of grownups can suddenly find themselves self-consumed, paranoid, disinterested, on edge, with eyes riveted on anything except the other *homo sapiens* next to them.

I am convinced that our behavior on an elevator tells us much about ourselves and what "growing up" does to us. Restrictive. Intimidating. Nerve-racking, at the worst. Awkward, at best. Confident people enter them and suddenly lose their sense of confidence. Friendly people enter and immediately become hesitant, reluctant, uncertain. Such a tense environment, such an awkward atmosphere.

And yet, let someone with an infant or baby enter. Let a child penetrate that icy chamber, and what happens is sheer magic.

One by one, the disengaged and disconnected eyes break rank and become intrigued with the countenance of a child. In a moment's time, faces brighten, voices emerge, and postures relax. With but the entrance of a youngster, the stilting code of conduct is injected with something far more compelling and much more appealing—the face of a child.

Unaware and unimpressed with anyone's rigid rules, a child's face rolls out a red carpet for weary souls and on-edge adults and says to us, "Relax. Everything's okay. You're here, I'm here, and that's just great!" A child's face, in such tedious moments, becomes a refuge, a haven, an oasis for the uptight. The presence of children can cut right through tense atmospheres. Their simple, eager innocence in a moment's time can redefine our lives and restore joy. Such an experience is at once a blessing and an indictment.

What's tragic is that what we find in the face of a child we have forgotten how to find in one another as adults, as men and women, as moms and dads. We could learn something from the children. A child's countenance willingly invites: "I'm glad you're here. I don't expect anything from you but just a smile or two. Let's enjoy this moment, each other's company, and not worry about anything else."

When most of us enter elevators, or step out into life itself for that matter, not only do the doors shut, our souls close up as well. However, when children enter, their uninhibited spirits have a way of prying ours open, if just but for one glorious moment.

Leading a little soul—a child—toward maturity is one of the most intriguing, challenging, and heart-stretching jobs we have ever had. It is amazing, exciting, and at times, incredibly overwhelming. There is something about the development of a child's will and ways that requires spiritual insight and sensitivity. No cookie-cutter process exists that just automatically works for every child. While the Bible certainly lays down absolutes for parents (i.e., "train up a child") it also includes big measures of mystery (i.e., "in the way he should go"). Parenting is challenging.

Whenever we take the time to genuinely and patiently observe the manner and insights of the children around us, we often find ourselves deeply intrigued, if not a bit envious. After all, there is such simplicity in a child's world, such wholehearted focus, such rapt attention at times, and such utter abandonment to whatever it is that has, for that moment at least, captured his or her interest.

There are two things always powerfully at work in raising children, and they are—did you guess it?—the will and the way. Shaping the will of a child is a monumental task, but so is guiding them in the right way. In order to help them in both areas, God made men and women with different propensities, both of which are invaluable to a child and to the parenting process.

The most quoted passage from the Bible on parenting is arguably Proverbs 22:6—"Train up a child in the way he should go, and when he is old he will not depart from it" (NKJV). Parenting is all about training children (or shaping their will) in the way they should go. A closer look at the original language used (Hebrew) and the meaning of this passage sheds more light. Some incredibly beautiful images and concepts emerge that can inform, equip, and inspire parents. Here are just a few:

"Train up"—the Hebrew word used here has two word pictures attached to it. One is of breaking a wild horse or stallion. Now there's a metaphor we parents can identify with on some days more than others, right? The other word picture is related to the process a Hebrew midwife in ancient Israel would use: putting a fruit paste in the mouth of a newborn in order to create a desire to nurse or feed soon after birth.

The two images of the wild stallion and the fruit paste seem so random and removed from each other, don't they? Yet, if these images are combined, a powerful concept emerges, an approach that can truly help a child grow in God's will God's way. It is this: *Parenting is all about taming a wild stallion by creating a taste in them for godliness!* Wise parents don't just push rules on their children, but they teach them within a relational context that is compelling and life giving.

Josh McDowell has wisely said for years that when it comes to parenting "rules without relationship leads to rebellion." From the first time we heard this concept, it has stayed with us and inspired and informed our parenting often.

"a child"—For years, whenever we heard or cited Proverbs 22:6, the "child" we envisioned was a little one, a toddler or elementary school child. But, the word used here for "a child" means truly *a child of any age*. Certainly, when children reach their adult years, parents need to release them to their own life and responsibility. Yet, in a sense, a dad never stops being a dad, a mom never stops being a mom, and a child never stops being a child. While oversight changes, love and faithful commitment to their well-being never should.

"in the way"—For a few years as parents, we considered "in the way" to mean "in our ways," "by the rules the parents determine," or even "by the Ten Commandments," etc. While certainly the Word of God is to be the foundation of the way we raise our children, there is something a bit more mysterious to this phrase.

The word used here for "in the way he should go" is literally referring to the "bents" or "unique patterns of interest" or "ways" that exist in your child—the "path" that God has uniquely placed within him or her and called him or her to. The word used here for "ways" is the same word used in Proverbs 30:19–20 when it says there are a few "ways too excellent for me to understand." The writer of Proverbs 30 is clearly caught up with some marvelous and amazing "ways" on earth that piqued his imagination and created a sense of wonder. He writes of things wondrous to watch and yet difficult to explain; so are the "ways" of children, their nature, and their unfolding life. Here's how he wrote it:

Three things are too wonderful for me;
four I do not understand:
the way *of an eagle in the sky,*
the way *of a serpent on a rock,*
the way *of a ship on the high seas,*
and the way *of a man with a maiden.*
(Proverbs 30:18–19 RSV, emphasis added)

A huge part of a parent's job, then, is to understand the unique "ways" or desires and gifts God has placed within a child.

"when he is old"—We used to think that this referred to some kind of dramatic deathbed conversion after a lifetime of rebellion as a child. But the Hebrew word is actually much more hopeful than that. It more closely means "the chin hanging down" or more likely, "when he is old enough to grow hair on his face." This points toward a much more powerful and hopeful sense of a parent's influence having effect from as early as adolescence on the way the child will live.

As it turns out, children benefit greatly in finding God's will and God's ways in their lives through the influence and involvement of their parents. A man's will and a woman's way can work wonders toward helping their children do God's will God's way.

Up Words and Down Words

Peggy Bert has suggested that it takes at least two positive words to offset the discouragement of just one negative word. Dr. John Gottman says the formula is closer to five-to-one for married couples.[27] And to be clear, what are some affirming things a dad or mom might say, things every child needs to hear? Here are a few of our favorites:

"I'm glad I get to be your dad/mom!"

"I sure love getting to spend time with you!"

"One of the things I like the best about you is. . ."

"I need a huge hug from you!"

"That was excellent. You did that really well!"

"You sure do look beautiful/handsome today!"

Genuine encouragement is soul food. Sowing sentences of support every day in the lives of your children will bolster their spirits and inspire their sense of confidence. It helps to engage their will and guide them on their way. Why would there be any reason, I ask, *not* to encourage our sons and daughters? The suppressing of much-needed encouragement has too often disheartened children, held back students, caged up creativity, embittered some, wounded others, and alienated many a child from his or her parent.

Gary Smalley says, "Affirming words from moms and dads are like light switches. Speak a word of affirmation at the right moment in a child's life and it's like lighting up a whole roomful of possibilities."[28]

Paul himself, for example, was careful with Timothy, his son in the faith, to applaud not only his accomplishments but also his person, his character. Just listen to Paul go on:

Timothy, you are like a son to me. (1 Timothy 1:2)
Oh, Timothy, you are God's man. (1 Timothy 6:11)
I know how much you trust the Lord. (2 Timothy 1:5)

Paul learned how to praise people face to face, in front of others, but he also learned to praise them behind their backs as he did when he wrote to the Philippians about this young man: "I have no one else like him, who will show genuine concern for your welfare. . . . But you know that Timothy has proved himself, because as a son with his father he has served with me in the work of the gospel" (Philippians 2:20, 22 NIV).

Parenting Well: Five *Ways* That Always *Will*

So how do parents raise their children up well, but still keep their souls open—open to them, open to God, and open to others? We have found at least five "ways" to parent our children. All of these have become tools of influence that can work wonders in opening and guiding our sons' and daughters' souls.

Soul Opener 1—The Time You Take

To make the most of a moment takes time, an investment of our lives and energy. Without a doubt, saying yes to time with our kids means saying no to some of the time we spend with other aspects of our lives—no to the job, no to the hobby, no to social media or television.

Pamela, for instance, created "Mom Adventure Days" with our kids, where from time to time she would randomly surprise them and pick them up early from school and take them out for some fun adventure. Also, we always took them out of school one day during the Christmas season for a family day of shopping and going to a new holiday movie.

Soul Opener 2—The Moments You Make

Even mud can make a moment. We found that out when my daughter Kristin was about three. Swimming in the ocean, I (Robert) reached into the water and scooped up some sand beneath the surface. Taking the mud, I smeared it all over my arm and said, "Kristin, do you know what this looks like?" She shook her head no. "That's what sin make our hearts look like," I returned.

"Wow," she said as her eyes widened.

"And do you know what Jesus' blood does?" I asked. As her head shook again, I plunged my arm deep into the water and brought it up just as quick, saying, "It washes it all away." She was instantly hooked with the metaphor. In fact, she insisted that I repeat the process at least a dozen times that day.

Years after I gave Kristin that mud-on-the-arm object lesson, something happened. While on vacation, I caught her, then twelve, telling the exact same story with my four-year-old son, Robbi, while they were swimming.

Life is full of teachable moments just waiting to be captured. The key as a parent is to stay open and to be spontaneous.

The one thing none of us can resist is genuine interest. Dale Carnegie once captured the principle in these words: "You can make more friends in two months by becoming genuinely interested in other people than you can in two years by trying to get other people interested in you."[29]

The fact is that most everyone loves to be asked about themselves, especially kids. Talk radio alone proves this. One of the most overlooked and underused tools in a parent's toolbox is great questions.

A while back, Dave, one of my dad friends, picked up his eleven-year-old daughter at school. Wanting to strike up an engaging conversation with her, he asked, "So, how was school today?"

"Okay," his daughter responded. And that was it. The car became awkwardly quiet (Know that feeling?). The question Dave asked, intended to engage his daughter and create interest, fell far short.

The problem was that the question fell flat. It was not sharp enough. It was unfocused. So I urged him just to tweak it a bit. After some encouragement, Dave gave it another shot. "So, what was the *best thing* that happened to you all day?" According to my friend, that sharpened question struck conversational gold. He and his daughter talked all the way home, and then some.

Talk show hosts spend hours sharpening questions in order to effectively engage the people they interview. Doesn't it make sense for us as parents to give some thought to what we're asking our kids and how we're going about it? The key is: *be interested*. It's downright irresistible.

A good question can open a conversation, but a great one can open a soul.

We both have strong memories, not of everything our fathers said, but of some things they said to us as children over and over again. Here are just a few:

> *"Robert, remember. . .always think before you speak."*
> *"Your grandfather kept the Crosby name good. I've tried to do the same. I expect you to do the same while you are away on this trip. It is up to you to keep a good name."*
> *"God did not promise you happiness, but joy and peace."*
> *"Any job worth doing is worth doing right."*
> *"Many a man has lost his soul over not controlling his sex drive."*
> *"When you start this job, remember. . .delegate, delegate, delegate. Don't try to do it all on your own."*

Apparently the psalmist also remembered the things his father said: "things we have heard and known, things our ancestors have told us. We will not hide them from their descendants; we will tell the next generation the praiseworthy deeds of the LORD, his power, and the wonders he has done" (Psalm 78:3–4 NIV).

The sayings of a father are, in essence, what comprise the majority of the book of Proverbs. It consists of hundreds of succinct statements of faith, value, and conviction that

Solomon used to pepper and prepare the souls of his children in order to teach them the ways of wisdom.

Pamela often says that nothing can take the place of the insights of a father. Her dad's consistent efforts at creating spontaneous family moments were anchor points in her childhood. We believe that God has designed the hearts of sons and daughters in such a way that they are incredibly influenced by the convictions and sayings of their dads.

The wise father understands that in order to raise faithful sons and daughters, he must *be devoted* to each of them. He must intentionally and consistently pass the nuggets of wisdom and insight he has learned. Godly parents put more than food on the table; they plant wisdom in their children's hearts.

SOUL OPENER 5—THE PROMISES YOU KEEP

When it is all said and done, kids need someone they can count on. Whenever we make a promise to our sons and daughters, we touch their souls. How? When we make a promise, we immediately create hope within them. Hope is a sacred thing. It is a motivator. It engages our faith in the possibility of a promise.

But when a promise is broken or unfulfilled, the results can be soul stripping. Consider this verse: "Hope deferred makes the heart sick, but a longing fulfilled is a tree of life" (Proverbs 13:12 NIV). But the right practices lead to incredible benefits (more on enjoying these in marriage in the next chapter).

The challenge we often face as parents is this: *be consistent.* Whenever we faithfully keep a promise, regardless of the cost, the results can be soul enlivening ("a tree of life"). A "promise fulfilled" builds a bridge not only into my child's life, but also into his or her soul. Not only does it encourage my son or daughter, it strengthens our relationship and paves a path for him or her toward a God who never fails to keep a promise.

Ask Up!

Questions for Will and Way Conversations

1. What did you think of the elevator rules at the start of the chapter? And what do these tell us about ourselves? Do you have any awkward elevator stories?

2. What aspect of the section on Proverbs 22:6 did you most connect with? How might you put this to work in your parenting?

3. Which ways do your children most value you "taking time" to be with them? What do you enjoy doing together?

4. What has been one of the most meaningful moments that you have shared with your child? What made that moment so memorable?

5. What is a "great question" to ask a child?

6. Can you recall a particular teachable moment in your child's life? How did you make the most of it?

7. When was a time that you did not keep a promise to your child? How did it affect your child and you?

PART III

Blending

Enjoying the Will and the Way

CHAPTER 11
The Teaming Couple

A successful marriage requires falling in love
many times, always with the same person.
                                   —Mignon McLaughlin

On the day of our tenth wedding anniversary, I (Robert) learned something, something powerful. But it took me ten years to learn it, ten years to see it. It happened while we were away on vacation.

To celebrate our tenth anniversary, Pamela and I took a trip to the countryside of Pennsylvania and used a friend's cottage. It was such a fun and relaxing time. Away from it all. Quiet. Wilderness. Alone together. Off the grid. No agenda.

The "lesson" came one day during our anniversary week. We had decided to divide our day into two parts, one indoors and the other outdoors. (By the way, since then, I have come to find out that Pamela's "ideal" day on vacation is one that consists of three parts.)

So, in the midst of part 1 of one of our days on our anniversary getaway, we were doing something I almost always enjoy—relaxing in a quiet spot while reading a good book. Pamela was lying on the bed in the bedroom reading, but through the door that opened to the living room she could see me on the couch doing the same thing.

While soaking up whatever page of the book I was reading at that time, all of a sudden I heard the biggest laugh coming out of the next room. I dropped my book, looked up, and said, "What in the world are you laughing about?"

Pamela was looking at me and just continued to laugh.

"I can't believe it!" she said.

"Can't believe what?" I asked.

"That we are doing this. I can't believe it," she returned.

"Doing what, reading?"

"Yes! Exactly," she said. "I am actually relaxing, reading, and believe it or not, having a good time. You know, ten years ago there was no way I would have enjoyed doing this."

"Really?" I asked.

"Absolutely. No way would I have done this on my vacation."

"So, what changed?" I asked.

"Being married to you," she said, smiling.

"Is that a fact? So, is that a good thing?" I asked.

"I think it is. Yeah, I really think it is," she said. "But, remember..."

"Oh, I know. I remember," I said. "The day isn't over yet."

Three or four hours later, we were out by a beautiful lake and walking along the shoreline. Pamela loves to walk the shore of lakes, beaches, and rivers and pull up rocks just to see what kind of ocean or lake life may exist underneath. Over the years, she has pulled out shells, clams, lobsters, crawfish—you name it, she has found it, and if there's a way to turn it into a pet, she has done so. Why, she has even had turtles confiscated at airports that she tried to smuggle from one state to another to add to her adventures.

A few minutes later, I pulled up a rock and found some other interesting creature to look at and talk about. When I did, suddenly I started laughing. I just couldn't help it. It just hit me.

"What are you laughing about?" Pamela asked.

"I can't believe it," I said.

"Can't believe what?" she asked.

"That we are doing this. I can't believe it," I returned.

"Doing what, wading in the water?" she asked.

"Yes! Exactly," I said. "I am actually out here looking under rocks with you and having a good time. There is no way I really would have enjoyed this so much ten years ago."

"Really?" she asked.

"No way," I said.

"So, what changed *you*?" she asked.

BLENDING

The third practice of the will and the way is this: *blending*. The scripture says of marriage: "they shall become one flesh" (Genesis 2:24 NKJV). In God's eyes, and in a spiritual sense, we believe that happens when a covenant is formed on the wedding day. But in a practical living-it-out sense, this union occurs little by little as we learn to serve each other in love and honor each other in life. It is a merging of lives and a mingling of souls. It takes a vow and a moment to start a marriage, but it takes a lifetime to build one.

The result of balancing and bending in marriage is a harmony of influence and a legacy of love; this is the *blending*. The process includes times of appropriately *asserting* yourself and other times of graciously *submitting* yourself to your partner. It is a rhythm of relational response that generally does not come naturally but must be learned. It is as delicate a process as learning how to dance together. However, the product is well worth the process—a deep and intimate marriage characterized by the blending of two souls.

Dan Montgomery describes a balanced soul as one that knows how to move almost rhythmically to what the need of the moment or the person in it calls for. He calls this pattern the Self-Compass.[30] It basically teaches that there are four key areas of response from which we need to respond: (1) strength, (2) weakness, (3) love, and (4) assertion. Each of these are important and vital. Here's how I describe them.

When you are responding to your spouse from the *strength* zone, your focus is on "what I have to offer." There are times that call on what we can bring to the table with confidence.

When you are responding to your spouse from the *weakness* zone, your focus is on "what I am lacking." These, are the times when we need to humbly acknowledge what we *don't have* to bring.

When you are responding to your spouse from the *love* zone, your focus is on "what you need." In these moments, your emphasis is on some need your spouse may have that you can serve and support.

Finally, when you are responding to your spouse from the *assertion* zone, your focus is on "what I want." These are those moments that call for decisiveness and determination.

No one of these zones is more "spiritual" than the other. In fact, we see examples of Jesus operating in each of them in the Gospels.

When it comes to men and women, *balancing* is the

potential you both bring to your relationship, *bending* is the commitment you make to your relationship, but *blending* is the glory God brings out in your relationship. It is what He makes out of it.

THE SYNC

According to research, through sharing life together couples become more alike and in sync even physiologically. Recent studies show that as we age in relationships, biological changes occur through which we become more like our partners than we were at the start of our relationship.

"Aging is something that couples do together," says Shannon Mejia, a research fellow at University of Michigan in Ann Arbor.[31] "You're in an environment together, and you're appraising that environment together, and making decisions together." She contends that through this process a couple becomes linked (or synced) physically, as well as emotionally. Perhaps this accounts for an older couple being able to finish each other's sentences.

Even one spouse's optimism can be physically advantageous to their partner. William Chopik, an assistant professor of psychology at Michigan State University, found that when one partner's optimism increases, the health of the other partner increases as well, showing up in fewer illnesses reported.[32] So, your spouse's optimism doesn't just lift your spirits—it improves your health.

Two Cultures

I (Pamela) was reminded of the process of building a marriage while I was helping my daughter plan her wedding. I had forgotten the time and effort that goes into finding the *dress* that encompasses everything a young woman dreams of. Beading or crystals? Straps or no straps? Sleeves or sleeveless? Mermaid style or bell shaped? So many decisions and attention to the details of a wedding day. My daughter mentioned to me that she thought for sure when she put on the dress that she would feel like a totally different person. A sign of too many Disney movies!

I have often said the enemy to the wedding planning process is the multiple editions of bridal magazines and Internet pictures posted after Photoshop and filters are applied! Everything looks so perfect, magical, dreamy, and romantic. It all portrays a mind-set that marriage is like being transported into this perfect "other" world of romantic perfection. The truth is, we strive to experience the fulfillment of oneness every day, but we never seem to actually or fully arrive. Oneness isn't the result of a beautiful, picture-perfect wedding, nor is it the product of a fabulous and exotic honeymoon, but the product of ongoing commitment of partnering through the dailies, the unexpected turns and embraceable moments.

If a person were to marry someone she had grown up with next door, it would still take the work of commitment and intentional discipline to experience the depth and joy of oneness. Why? Because the two families and backgrounds are two different cultures with two different ways they celebrate life—two different types of traditions, values, and beliefs.

TWO CHRISTMASES

I will never forget our first Christmas as a newly married couple. At this point I had thoroughly enjoyed being married and off on our own, building our own independent life. My parents were in Michigan and Robert's were in South Carolina, while we were living in upstate New York working at a church with inner-city youth and having the time of our lives.

My Northern family always celebrated Christmas at night on Christmas Eve. Life with my pastor-dad, mom, and two brothers was full of Christmas fun and surprises. Earlier on Christmas Eve my dad would take me shopping in the snow on a daddy-daughter date to pick out Mom's last-minute shopping gift from him. After attending Christmas Eve service, we would race home for Christmas.

The Krist family Christmas would begin with a delicious and well-thought-out hot meal, and then my dad would read the Christmas story from scripture and soon begin the process of opening gifts. Every gift was wrapped and handed out one by one. We would often play jokes on each other as a part of the night, and we would ooh and aah over the handmade gifts. This would often take us late into the night, but the memories were embedded in our minds and hearts.

Soon after marriage I experienced my first Southern Crosby family Christmas.

In my husband's family were his mom, dad, and younger brother. Robert couldn't wait to take me home to experience our first Christmas as a married couple with his family. Even though the trees had some leaves and the grass would still be a bit green, Robert's mom would make every effort to make everything feel so Christmas-y by decorating the house from the ceiling to the floor. The smell of traditional Crosby cookies turned my strong adult husband into a little boy excited about being home for Christmas. The Crosby home would often be full of people I didn't know, and I endeavored to fit in as the new and only "daughter." Though there weren't any beautiful white snowfalls, Christmas was definitely in the air. What I wasn't ready for was the shock to my system of experiencing a whole new set of family traditions, starting with no Christmas Eve service, no Christmas story read, and no traditional meal. Christmas was going to be celebrated on Christmas morning, and I was told to be prepared; it would be early. Everything I knew and had loved about my childhood Christmases was about to change.

Christmas morning came, and we were woken up before our 7:00 a.m. alarm went off with "It's Christmas!" We all ran into the family room, where the Christmas tree was lit and gifts were lying under the tree. Some were wrapped, and some were not wrapped—they were "naked gifts"—quite a shock to my Yuletide Yankee system. *Hmmmm, that's okay*, I thought. *I can do this. I'm a big girl.*

Once we were all standing around in the family room, I heard something like, "Go get 'em!" and suddenly Christmas paper was ripping and flying all over the place, bodies were jumping over each other grabbing gifts like little boys retreating to their childhood. Someone yelled, "Hey, this one's for you!" and with that a box was thrown my way. Christmas took a whole ten minutes. Gifts were all over the floor, and everyone was saying, "Thank you" while I was left trying to collect myself with a pile of Christmas wrap at my feet. We then went into the kitchen and enjoyed some scrambled eggs and traditional sausage biscuits. I did my best to keep it together. After a few more minutes, I excused myself and went into the bedroom to call and wish my Michigan family Merry Christmas.

The sound of my mom's voice melted me to tears. I tried hard to hide it as they proceeded to tell me about their great Christmas Eve service; Dad told me how much he missed our shopping date and how he felt so sad shopping alone. The quiet tears turned into Niagara Falls all over my face. Two cultures, two sets of traditions, two sets of expectations created an explosion of emotions instead of being overwhelmed with a blending of newly married oneness.

Honeymoon 2.0

Instead of marriage being the overnight honeymoon miracle I originally expected, marriage instead is a daily living miracle through the process of blending two completely different lives, learning together through the high and not-so-high points of life. The experience of blending two lives into one is like putting two different countries on an uninhabited planet and expecting them to become one overnight.

The result of balancing and bending in marriage is a harmony of influence and a legacy of love; this is the *blending*. The process includes times of appropriately *asserting* yourself and other times of graciously *submitting* yourself to your partner. It is a rhythm of relational response that generally does not come naturally but must be learned. Remember, it is as delicate a process as learning how to dance together. However, the product is well worth the process—a deep and intimate marriage characterized by the blending of two souls.

By the way, Christmas is still full of traditions for our current Crosby family of three daughters, a son, a son-in-law, and just this month, a brand-new grandson as we have taken our favorite childhood memories and blended them to create the most loved holiday in our household. Christmas Day begins early with a big breakfast full of traditional and well-planned dishes, including South Carolina traditional cookies and sausage balls. We follow up a beautiful Christmas meal together with a traditional reading of the Christmas story in poem form and a hot-and-cold game of "who can find baby Jesus." Once the ceramic baby is discovered and put in His manger, Christmas gifts can begin! It's an all-day celebration of blended family traditions and memories, but one gift at a time.

Culture Shock

My (Robert here) great awakening during my first Christmas with Pamela's family was how many gifts of all sizes they gave to each other at Christmas—each one individually wrapped and many bedecked with bows and ribbons. They even write cards to each other and read aloud every word—*every* word. And only one gift is opened by one person at a time while everyone else watches and takes videos/photos. All in all, opening gifts takes hours to complete. And imagine adding grandchildren to the mix.

For the first couple of years, this process was quite an

adjustment. As one of just two boys in our family, as Pamela said earlier, I was used to a rapid-fire, rip-'em-open quick Christmas morning. As kids, the goal was to get them open so we could play with the toys. So the slower approach at first felt like watching a slow-motion movie, in slower motion. As Pamela says, I had to learn to slow down and embrace the moment.

Pamela and I still find our default mode is to focus on our individual wants and to overlook each other's needs all too easily. In the next two chapters, we will look more closely at the deepest needs of men and of women.

THE DIVINE DANCE

Christian marriage calls us to not only slow down, but perhaps more so to enter a slow dance of sorts. The dance of the will and the way is reminiscent and reflective of the relationship that exists among the members of the Trinity. In this sense the marriage union is a picture of "as in heaven, so on earth" (Matthew 6:10), of "your kingdom come, your will be done" and of "where two or three of you come together in my name, I am there" (Matthew 18:20). In fact, some of the earliest Christian theologians described the relationships of the members of the Trinity as a dance, especially of a "circle dance."

> *In the seventh century, John of Damascus, a*
> *Greek theologian, described the relationship of*
> *the persons of God (Trinity) as* perichoresis.
> *Perichoresis means literally "circle dance."*
> Choros *in ancient Greek referred to a round*

dance performed at banquets and festive occasions. The verb form, choreuo, *meant to dance in a round dance. (These round dances often included singing, hence the English word* chorus.) *The prefix* peri *(Greek for round about or all around) emphasized the circularity of the holy dance envisioned by John. Based on the biblical descriptions of Father, Son and Spirit, John depicted the three persons of the Trinity in a circle. A perichoretic image of the Trinity is that of the three persons of God in constant movement in a circle that implies intimacy, equality, unity, and yet distinction among the various members and love.*

Theologian Shirley Guthrie calls this image of God a "lovely picture that portrays the persons of the Trinity in a kind of "choreography" (Greek choros-graphy*), similar to ballet. In this circle dance of God is a sense of joy, freedom, song, intimacy, and harmony. "The oneness of God is not the oneness of a distinct, self-contained individual; it is the unity of a community of persons who love each other and live together in harmony.*[33]

Today we have our own traditions culled from a blend of the Crosby and Krist traditions with a few of our own added. But for the record, we do practice the slow-motion gift opening. I took a hint from God's advice to Abraham: "'Do whatever Sarah tells you'" (Genesis 21:12 NLT). (I couldn't resist!)

Two different lives from two different cultures are how we started. We experienced some culture shock at first and had to negotiate along the way, but we have found that marriage is a process of growing and changing. If we are willing to value the differences and bend where needed, then there can come a blending together.

"These two shall become one"...but not overnight!

ASK UP!
Questions for Will and Way Conversations

1. Since you were first married, are there ways in which you and your spouse have changed through your influence on each other? How have your lives "blended"?

2. What did you think of Robert and Pamela's different experiences in celebrating Christmas? Can you identify? What differing Christmas traditions did you bring into your marriage and family?

3. How do your differences as a couple *balance* you in your lives together?

4. What are some ways you have had to learn to *bend* toward each other's strengths in order to make your marriage stronger?

5. Was your introduction to your spouse's family a bit of a "culture shock"? How so?

6. What did you think of the description of the Trinity as a "divine dance"?

7. In what ways can your marriage reflect the nature of God to you and your spouse and to your children?

CHAPTER 12
What Men Want Most!

Every man is a volume if you know how to read him.

—William Ellery Channing

If a man could change two things about his marriage, what would they be? Well (Robert here), according to Gottmann's extensive research on men, the top two responses were consistent and emphatic and, of course, stated in just a few words. At first glance, they may not sound very "spiritual," but to men they are vital. Here they are, in their words: "less fighting" and "more sex."[34] That's right. Leave it to a man to provide such sweeping relational diagnosis in only four words and short ones, at that.

Perhaps a more intriguing way to say this is they want more peace in their marriage and more physical intimacy with their wives. While some men get pegged by women as "animals," just wanting and thinking about sex all the time, many men do live in their marriages with frustrations over the conflicts and lack of connection that exist.

Men are often more quietly insecure and even desperate in some areas of life than they will ever let on. Add to that an indomitable ego, and you have a lethal mixture of the soul. Henry David Thoreau, a mind who reflected much on life, observed, "Most men lead lives of quiet desperation and go to the grave with the song still in them." So, ladies, although men will likely read this chapter as well, while you read it, try to do so in order to understand him rather than find something "wrong" with him. You may, in fact, find that some of those things about him that frustrate you the most are not just true about him but also about men in general. While that may not remove your disappointment, it may adjust your expectations.

The challenge and the opportunity of reading a chapter such as this one is what you will do with the information you discover. Will you consider it, reject it, or use it against him? Choose wisely and read on.

A DIFFERENT WAY TO SPELL LOVE

The thing men want the most is often quite different than what women most want. As wonderful and romantic and celebrated as *love* is, at the core of their souls men do not primarily want to be "loved," at least not in the sense that many women understand it; rather, they want to be respected and honored. Because they are so connected to their will, generally speaking, they are more *volitional* than *emotional* in their orientation. Whether the reasoning for this is primarily physiological or sociological is arguable. Still, the fact remains that it is a practical reality that shows up in most marriages, in many relationships between men and women at home and at work, and in numerous studies.

At his core, a man's will desires respect. While at its worst a man's will may sometimes demand this respect, the fact is that the woman who desires to tap into a need deep in her man's soul will be wise to pay attention to this. To use

Thoreau's language, respect summons the "song" in a man. Just as when women are listened to (or "attended" to), they feel loved; so, when men are respected, that makes them also feel loved.

Men care more about honor and admiration than they do about love. Paul reveals his understanding of this in the book of Ephesians when he admonishes women to "submit yourselves to your own husbands" (Ephesians 5:22 NIV). This is not a command for a woman to become a slave or doormat for her husband to walk on. No, on the contrary, Paul was reflecting the understanding of a man's nature through inspiration and how very much a man desires to be admired, honored, and respected. In fact, the context of the book of Ephesians is Paul's teaching on "submit[ting] to one another out of reverence for Christ" (Ephesians 5:21 NIV). God knows that to a man, admiration, respect, and honor do equate *being loved*.

The lifestyle of relationships and roles portrayed by Paul in Ephesians 5 and Peter in 1 Peter 3 is controversial today, and many people, including some Christians, react to them and almost want to simply dismiss these passages. Yet, in order to appreciate and understand them, we must rise above our hierarchically challenged society and reimagine Eden, a place full of intimacy, trust, and love prior to the fall of man.

It is impossible to appreciate Pauline or Petrine insights on relationships if viewed in light of the values of a fallen culture. One must imagine a kingdom culture, one full of faith and absent of fear. This is why Peter speaks so forthrightly about Sarah's willing submission to Abraham and insists to Christian wives that "you are her daughters if you do what is right and do not give way to fear" (1 Peter 3:6 NIV).

The kingdom of God's values and culture are paradoxical and counterintuitive to our natural understanding of what seems "fair" and "normal." That is because so many of our values and social senses are rooted in fear—fear of failure, fear of being taken advantage of, and fear of inferiority. But in the kingdom of God "the last will be first and the first will be last" (Matthew 20:16 NIV), the "greatest one" among us is the one who serves (Matthew 23:11), and the ones who "humble" themselves are the ones God will ultimately exalt (1 Peter 5:6–7).

Paul's teaching on submission is a sophisticated multidimensional revelation of a keen understanding of the nature of a man's soul. Throughout his exhortation, Paul is acknowledging that the way to a man's heart and soul is through learning what it takes to help him feel admired, even honored. The challenge, however, for men and women is that *we too often tend to focus much more on how our spouse needs to love us than on how we need to love them*; we focus more on what we get than what we give. Paul was giving us a great marriage insight here. In part, he was saying: *The way to engender love in the heart of a man is for his wife to show him honor and admiration.* Make room for his will and he will feel like you are making room for him.

Who's Taking Out the Garbage?

We (Pamela here) have all grown up with a certain picture in our minds and hearts that defines "marriage." For instance, in some marriages the man cooks, while in others the kitchen is solely the wife's domain. Who oversees the finances is also different from one marriage to another—or who takes out the garbage, for that matter.

In some marriages the woman appears more driven than the man, and in others they are like two ships moving fast but in different directions. As mysterious as each marriage is, there are some foundational blocks that appear to be the same no matter what roles the man or the woman takes on. As we have considered thus far, women have a way about them and men have a will. For instance, you may have tried to help around the house and heard the words, "Don't stack the dishes that way!" or "Look, this is the way I like the dishes placed in the dishwasher" or "This is the way the mail should be processed" or "Don't you know the kitchen rules?" Or no matter how much reasoning you may give, the ladies may have heard their husband's will saying, "I told our son 'no' the first time and I still mean 'no'! Nothing's changed!" Yet, they may often have no idea of just why their spouse said 'no'.

As mysterious as the way of a woman is to a man, so is the will of a man mysterious to a woman, regardless of who takes out the garbage or cooks in the kitchen. There is something about the determination of a man and the way a woman cares that is simply woven into the fabric of who we are. It was many years into our marriage until I realized this and saw that, generally speaking, men often value receiving love through affirmations. Speaking words of affirmation to your man doesn't mean he has to be perfect or that he has perfectly met all of your expectations. Sometimes affirming is important because he is simply a human being who needs to hear when he is getting it right, or at least close to right, *right*?

NAVIGATING THE WILL OF A MAN: TEN PIECES OF "INSIDE INFORMATION" WOMEN NEED TO KNOW

I (Robert here) compiled these observations below from several years of observing and counseling men and women. The insights comprise similar themes that appear in numerous surveys, lists, and interactions—things I have studied and others I have developed. While not all scientific in nature, they represent general insights and convictions that regularly strike a chord with men. While men often fail at communicating these motivations or "emotions" or "he-motions," they are the very things that often weigh on a man's mind and heart.

Navigating the will of a man and the way of a woman requires curiosity and interest. Ladies, it's time to pick up your husband's eyeglasses and look for a few minutes through the lenses with which he sees and feels life and his relationships, including his relationship with you. Here is a partial list of things we men wish that women could catch.

Your man wishes you would:

- *Understand that. . .* **He really wants to make you happy, but** *often* **isn't sure just quite how to do so.** If there were a "joy box" he could open in your soul every day and a combination to open the lock, he would likely make that one of his first steps. Gottman's research found, "Men also want less conflict. Way less conflict. [Men] don't want to be the source of her unhappiness, and when she's unhappy, [they] want to fix whatever's broken and move on. Men feel responsible for women's feelings. And this is where men go way, way wrong."[35]

- *Understand that. . .* **Most men are not as in touch with their emotions as women; actually they often find them a bit scary.** Your moods are often one of the most challenging things in his world for him to navigate. And the fact that you process the emotional aspects of life in depths he often cannot comprehend makes stepping into those waters sometimes more intimidating than you may know. While women often tend to examine their emotions, men tend to simply act on them. Your anger can suffocate him.

- *Understand that. . .* **It's not** *what* **you say; it's more about** *the way* **you say it.** In his mind, in order for you to have a "way with words," remember less is usually more. Use fewer words, but make each one count. Your calm complaint will get more of his attention than a loud, angry one. If you rehearse your disappointments with him, you will make him feel defeated. But if speak of your trust, you will make him feel responsible.

- *Understand that. . .* **Men enjoy romance when it is working but often question just how to get it started.** If "romance" equals relational intimacy, then he likes it when a loving tone exists between the two of you. While he doesn't want you to behave in a "needy" manner, he wants a relational warmth to exist between you. It may seem like he does not want romance in the relationship, but in all likelihood he wants it more than you know but in different ways than you may expect. Since men are generally more independent than women, they often don't convey a need to be needed. But when it comes to romance and relational warmth, they often don't know when to try their hand at it and if their efforts will be effective. Gottman's research found "that men actually want more intimacy just as much as women, but they feel that intimacy when there's less fighting and more sex."[36]

- *Understand that. . .* **Your affirmations work wonders on his *will*.** Men value affirmation. They appreciate being appreciated, honored, and respected. The wise wife will affirm everything that is "affirmable" in her husband and will catch him doing things *right*. For men, affirmation is love.

- *Understand that. . .* **He desires to display his strengths in front of you and in the context of your relationship.** Do you remember how much your husband appreciated how you made over him and the things he did when you first started dating? Do you remember how "strong" he was when he picked you up and hugged you? How "smart" he was when he told you all about some subject he was interested in? How "thoughtful" he was when he got you the gift you "really wanted" (whether it really was the one you "really wanted" the most or not)? Those moments and those affirmations are part of what made him fall for you. He may be a bit older now, but that is a likely "song" in his soul just waiting to be summoned by you as only you can.

- *Understand that. . .* **Men crave admiration and honor more than love; in fact, to them, admiration is love.** John Eldredge notes "a man aches for affirmation, for validation, to know that he has come through. This also explains his deepest fear—failure."[37] For a man the "Love Equation" is this: *Respect + Admiration = True Love.* Also, sometimes a man's anger in the home may be a reaction to feeling disrespected. Instead of telling him he doesn't listen well enough, try communicating in ways he will more likely hear. That doesn't mean you should not confront him. If needed, confront his will but do so in an honoring way. Gottman found that "in a more general way, a man wants to be desired and to feel like the woman in his life wants him, adores him, and approves of him just the way he is."[38]

- *Understand that. . .* **He sees the goal of conversation differently than you; to him it is about "getting the report."** Research by Deborah Tannen showed the "goal of conversation" for men is different than for women.[39] While men focus on getting the *report*, women focus on gaining the *rapport* of connection and understanding. When a man hears about a problem, he wants to solve or fix it as quickly as possible. His brain is hardwired for that.

- *Understand that. . .* **Men don't like to be surprised by sudden emotional "channel changes."** In other words, while neurological studies affirm that women, generally speaking, have an advantage on processing and understanding emotions from the early stages of life, most men do not. Thus when they are in a certain relational "mode" with their wives, they are not apt to quickly adapt to sudden changes. For example, if they are enjoying a simple after-dinner romantic walk with their wife, this is not a time for her to confront him over some tense issue. Scott Stanley, a codirector for the Center for Marital and Family Studies at the University of Denver, says, "This is not time to work out differences. When they should be in fun and friendship mode, [some people] switch into problem and conflict mode."[40] His advice is simple: *Don't mix modes!*

- *Understand that. . .* **He wants to have *his way* with you more often than you may know.** No matter what your level of sexual activity or intimacy is in your marriage, the odds are that he probably wants to have sex with you more than you realize. And Gottman's research showed that the most fulfilling sexual experiences for men and women are the holistic connections of "the mind, the heart and the genitals." With sexual intimacy, it is not so much about what you do as the way you do it.[41]

The wife who takes time to "study her man" and understand what he deeply desires is well on her way to enriching her marriage. In the next chapter we will find out more about how a man can do the same for his wife.

Ask Up!
Questions for Will and Way Conversations

1. Generally speaking, in what ways are men's and women's needs the most similar?

2. In what ways are the needs of men and women different?

3. What does it require for a woman to truly and deeply discern the needs of a man?

4. Do we tend to assign certain duties in our minds to men and others to women (i.e., taking out the garbage or mowing the lawn)? Are masculinity and femininity really defined by such things?

5. Do men and women tend to process their emotions differently, generally speaking? Explain.

6. What makes respect and admiration so important to a man? What are ways that women can best convey this?

7. Do you identify with the suggestion that men tend to look at conversation as a "report" while women focus more on "rapport"? How so?

CHAPTER 13
What Women Deeply Desire!

You know you're in love when you can't fall asleep because reality is finally better than your dreams.

—Dr. Seuss

I don't do as much people watching as my mom. When I was a little girl, I knew she could sit just about anywhere and be entertained by watching all kinds of people and even imagining what their conversations may be about. I do, however, catch myself at times watching the magnetic influence a women's way can have on men—so much so it can turn heads.

For instance, have you ever been in a mall right in front of a woman's clothing store and seen a group of men just sitting and waiting? They join the other appointed watchmen of the shopping bags, not so convinced that it will only take "a couple of minutes" to see if maybe *this* store has what the wife or girlfriend is shooooooopping for. (My husband tells me—"women shop" and "men hunt.") These men gather outside the store while she tries on a couple dozen outfits. They do this instead of awkwardly walking with her in the store and repeatedly asking, "How much longer do we need to be in here?"

Made up of many ages, these men in waiting keep themselves amused with a variety of activities. Some young dads are taking care of their little ones who are running around, giving Mommy some "me time." There are usually a couple of men glued to their phones, checking their stocks, texting their buddies about tee time, watching a movie, reading a book, or getting caught up with the news. Coffee in hand, they are single focused until the woman's purchases are made and they can finally get to lunch.

Just about that time there comes along—*that* woman. You know which one I'm talking about, right? The one every other woman can't stand.

It's that woman with the right-sized hips to go with the right clingy outfit and the perfumed fragrance that lingers as she and her long, bouncy hair saunter by. Then—one by one the spell is cast. Men stop texting. Another shifts in his seat and sits up a bit straighter. Little children fall down, but Daddy doesn't notice. He is in another orbit.

Mr. Slick quickly puts his sunglasses on in hopes his glaring and staring don't get him into trouble (sort of obvious when you're wearing the sunglasses indoors!).

What is it? What magnetizes their sudden interest? Is it her figure, her movement, her style, her fragrance? I'm sure any man reading this right now is screaming with their indoor voices, "Yes! Yes! Yes! It's all of the above and more!" They probably don't even remember what her face looks like, right? They have that "I just can't help myself" glaze all over their faces.

As the woman continues to walk beyond them, heads begin to turn, they shift their bodies in her direction and watch the movement like that of a rhythmic creature creating a trance. And then, just as suddenly they hear an all-too-familiar voice: "Honey! Honey! Didn't you get my text? Can you come in the store? I think I found *the* outfit! I want to show you. . . Will you come in and tell me what you think of it? But take off those sunglasses. . . You won't see anything with those on!"

Oh yeah?

The spell is broken, but the scene all too familiar.

AMAZING WAYS

Women have been referred to as residents of the Planet Venus (i.e., *Men Are from Mars and Women Are from Venus*, John Gray, 1992), as spaghetti (*Men Are Like Waffles and Women Are Like Spaghetti*, Bill and Pam Farrel, 2001), as teabags (i.e., *"A woman is like a teabag; you never know how strong she is until she's in hot water."*—Eleanor Roosevelt, 1944), and the list goes on.

Though these and other word pictures have been somewhat helpful in understanding the general design and differences of men and women, one thing remains true: a woman is like nothing else we can compare her with.

Just consider yourselves, women. (Bear with us for a few sentences, men. You may need to hear this, too!) Ladies— there are some things you have that are uniquely yours. For instance:

> *Your curves*—no matter the size, men like curves.
>
> *Your gifts and abilities*—they are in action and, as confirmed by the latest brain science, functioning on multiple layers simultaneously.
>
> *Your love that flows so fully through your veins*—just

waiting for the next moment so you can give or get a hug or kiss, soothe a child's fears, or feed a hungry soul with care and concern.

Your mind—and curiosity that hungers for new information.

Your heart—that longs for places yet to be discovered.

You're so gifted—you can cook an amazing meal and at the same time help your child with the next spelling test, while texting your mom, sister, or BFF to see how her day was.

You are just so altogether amazing! Intricate. Delicate. Strong of spirit. Graceful. Valuable. Dedicated. Passionate. Creative. Colorful. Lively. Adventurous. Fun. Disarming. Playful. Energetic. Hopeful. Loving. Alluring.

WOMAN OF INFLUENCE

My dad, Dave, has been married to my mom, Shirley, for sixty-plus years and pastored churches diligently with Mom at his side for fifty of them. Informed by their faith and traditional values, without question Dad has been and continues to be the head of the home, with Mom serving sweetly beside him. Yet, they have mutually encouraged each other along their journey toward oneness.

Nonetheless, I have so often heard my dad say in his unmistakable voice, "Shirley is amazing! Honestly, I wish I had the influence and power of a woman!"

Truth be known, most of us women wish we more fully understood just how much of that "powerful influence" we actually do have. Sometimes we doubt and question it. Though there are some similarities with men, women are uniquely and differently designed individuals, and they desire to be deeply appreciated and valued as such. None of them, not one, wants to be lumped into some category of "estrogen-saturated, mindless females." They need to be reminded of their value and often.

COUNT THE WAYS

Have you ever noticed how unique and individual the ways of a woman are? Let's start with some smaller daily "ways" you may *not* have noticed. Then again, maybe you have. For example, if you have five different women show you how they fold their bathroom towels, what will you find? *Five* different ways to fold a towel—that's what.

For years I thought all women folded towels the way my mom taught me. There was only *one* way my mom wanted a towel folded. Any other way I tried would just get shaken out, and we'd start over again learning the "right way" to fold one. But what was it that made Mom's way the "right way"?

There was a reason.

You see, Mom knew just the way the closet would look when the towels were folded right-sized and stacked up on top of one another. Mom's way kept the closet looking neat and organized, maximizing every inch of storage room without taking up too much space. In our home, it was always the three-fold way. Guess what? I still fold my towels that way and have taught my family the same.

The conflict came when my mother-in-law used the two-fold way to fold, so I can always tell when my husband has been helping with the laundry. The example is a simple one, but it's only one of a woman's many *ways*. Each and every one of them represents something about her, something she cares about.

Women also typically have a specific way of folding fitted sheets (I still struggle with that one!), a specific way we like to vacuum a room (with or without the lines?), a way we like dishes stacked in the dishwasher or how we wrap a gift (or decide to skip the wrap and just grab a bag). When you think of it and begin to count the ways we prefer our lives to be lived and the ways we want them to look, the list is virtually endless. There's the *way* we like to look, the *way* we like our homes to function, the *way* we like our children to behave, and the *way* we love to be loved.

Women just have a "way" about them that is mysterious, compelling, and alluring enough to write countless songs about (just ask Billy Joel). The wise man will be aware of his woman's ways. It is even something about her way that captures the attention and heart of a man, causing him to commit himself to her "for as long as we both shall live."

His Will Complements Her Way

Men, when was the last time you noticed some little thing she did as one of her unique ways, not as something simply "annoying to you? Can you list three to five of her ways that make her unique to you?

What could be the possible outcome of showing her that you value her ways? It could be you secretly admire her way of creating memories, leading a team, decorating your house; her way of organizing calendars or finances, reading the emotional temperature of a room, caring for her parents or yours; or is it her way of loving your children? Go ahead. Let the secret out of the bag! Tell her about it.

What could possibly happen to your relationship if you took a little time and placed a spotlight of honor on her and one or two of her amazing ways? Do it in front of your family, your children, or friends. Remember, her ways are different than yours, some of them *so* different, which is why you fell in love with her in the first place.

Your compliments, your actions that prove your love once again, or just a simple arm around her waist can make all the difference. Add to it a few whispered words like "I love the way you. . ." "I've thought of the way you love me all day; I couldn't think of anything else," or "Your love for me is such a beautiful example to our children." These types of words will soften the hard shell of distrust and protection. Negative words and experiences that enable such a shell include, but are not limited to: personal disappointments, negative self-talk, and past memories that destroy and disfigure what love desires to build.

When a man begins to take the time to understand and truly appreciate that the ways of the woman are not there to reduce him and compete with him, progress is made. When a man realizes that a woman's ways are intended to bring an even greater depth of life to his, it will develop something brand new for him. He will discover a new level of connection and intimacy, a patience and concern, fostering a spirit of commitment and protection toward the woman he loves. It is then that a man's will can confidently and lovingly lead the way of the woman into a realm of safety and trust and provide her with an opportunity to emerge as God has intended.

> *By wisdom a house is built, and through under-standing it is established; through knowledge its rooms are filled with rare and beautiful trea-sures.*
>
> (Proverbs 24:3–4 NIV)

TABLETALK

Not long ago, I enjoyed a conversation about a woman's ways with some amazing women in California at the kitchen table over coffee and pie (my four faves: these women + CA + key lime + coffee). Once again, I was reminded of the similarities we share in this sisterhood and in being women. We come from a variety of ages, backgrounds, hometowns, and occupations, and though our daily routines are quite different, our hopes, dreams, and desires within marriage were pain-fully similar. The reason I use the word *painfully* is because at times there were tons of pain as we reflected on our original hopes, youthful dreams, and some of our marital delusions.

The question we started with was: "What is it you believe women desire most?"

The answers came swiftly, were close to the surface, and resonated deeply among the group. Though you would think the answers would be centered more on a lack of intimacy or challenges in identity, instead the answers put a big spotlight on a woman's desire for something else: *security*.

Some of the responses included:

- "I don't desire anything different today than what caused me to fall in love with my husband originally—a sense that this was someone I could trust, feel safe with, find security in."
- "I felt protected, and that stole my heart."
- "I desire safety and financial security, meaning no matter what occurs in life, if I get sick, if we face financial emergencies, if I gain weight, he will stay with me through life's unexpected ups and downs."
- "I believe women desire someone they can really feel safe with, for the long haul."
- "I desire a trust and commitment that goes so deep that other relationships cannot threaten what we have."

In a nutshell, research confirms that women desire:
Security (trust)
Protection
Intimacy

A WOMAN'S THREE DESIRES

A man's will is designed by God to provide some of the things a woman desires most. This, however, always requires engagement and intentionality. Once again, these desires include security, protection, and intimacy. Let's consider each of them briefly.

There have been many times my daughters or other young adult women have asked me the age-old question, "How did you know when you really fell in love. . .the committed kind of love?"

I usually tell them that I surprised myself. I had thought "falling in love" meant a rush of emotions, firework-like heart-throbbing flashes of "Oh my gosh—he takes my breath away!" But instead I was overwhelmed with a different rush; rather, I found a deep sense of safety and peace with Robert. This young man's presence brought calmness to my otherwise topsy-turvy anxieties and insecurities. I had a deep sense of security whenever we were together. I could share my thoughts and secrets, my fears and concerns.

We met our senior year of college when my sights were already set on life after graduation. As a female, I was extremely anxious about my life. Like a boat swaying out on the ocean, I needed to count on an anchor of sorts, a man who would bring a certain steadiness. I wanted an anchor in my life to provide a "staying" power, no matter how much I am tossed around by all the uncertainties of life. I simply wanted to know that he would remain steady, consistent, and faithful. For the first time in my young adult life, safety, protection, and security felt like a truer and deeper love than emotional or even physical fireworks.

But how can a man provide a sense of security at the level a woman desires? To a woman the answer is quite basic: *communicate with honesty.*

A woman longs to understand the heart of her husband. While sexually he wants to be brought "inside" of her, emotionally she wants to be brought "inside" of him. Gottman's research shows that for the woman, *emotional* closeness helps her desire sexual intimacy with her husband; while *sexual* intimacy helps him feel more emotionally close to her. She desires to be drawn into the secret places of his life and thoughts. Honest communication is as if her husband has handed her the key to his heart and draws her closer, inviting her to take on the role of a trusted confidante.

Open communication regarding something as simple as a man's daily concerns, all the way to his debilitating fears or temptations, in a strange and mystical way uncovers his soul and creates a space for oneness to take place at a deep emotional level for the woman; a place to be "naked and unashamed" (Genesis 3:25). This allows her to enter into a place of honor and safety, posting a Do Not Enter sign for the rest of the world. This level of transparency communicates that the man values his wife's insights, her wisdom, and that he trusts in her. Gary Smalley writes to men, "Make it your goal to create an environment that feels like the safest place on earth."[42]

When men don't communicate their concerns openly and honestly, they are often blinded to the silent insecurities they create as a result in the woman. A man's will too often convinces him that if he doesn't uncover his soul and talk about the issue then maybe she won't see or feel them or discover any weakness in him at all. This becomes emotionally disabling for her. Her womanly ways tell her, in one form or another, "It's not safe right now," and her desire for safety and security begins to fade. A chasm on the path to oneness begins to develop.

The man becomes isolated and detached when he pulls back; she begins to close her soul as well. When a man's will covers his soul, it creates a silence and detachment. With the hope that he is simply "protecting" his bride from the truth, she senses danger and begins to protect herself instead. This could include secretly making financial decisions, developing new relationships, pouring herself into her work or her children's lives, and more.

PROTECTION—A MAN'S WILL *TO GUARD*

In the middle of our kitchen table conversation in California, another question was posed that day: Can women sabotage what they desire most?

Absolutely!

We do it more often than we like to admit. For instance, many women want a strong husband (more about that in the next chapter), but one who is gentle enough to change a baby's diaper. They want a man who is independent and yet a partner; someone who is decisive, but also takes time to hear her desires; a man who leads the family while considering everyone else's wishes. Women want a husband who makes exciting vacation plans to exotic Facebook-worthy places without using up their savings account; a husband who doesn't live to work but also doesn't take off so many days that he may lose his job. Rod Cooper calls these paradoxical expectations "the double-binds of manhood."[43]

Though a woman desires protection, she also must be able to discern his attempts at providing it. This may not always appear the way she pictured protection would look. Maybe she is quiet and shy, and his protection sounds a bit too loud and aggressive. Or perhaps she appears more confident on the outside and comfortable with an in-your-face approach, and his style of protection is one of reasoning together, remaining calm and controlled. It is important to remember what is at the heart of the person and situation. His efforts must be acknowledged and appreciated, not scrutinized and judged.

Intimacy—a Man's Will *to Be Relationally Engaged*

On the topic of intimacy, I would like to toss a white flag in the air on behalf of the men. This is not to indicate the beginning of a flag football game but rather a flag with an "SOS" printed on it for all men to see. This SOS is a reminder of what one of the wisest men on earth understood and recorded in the Song of Solomon. A woman's intimate ways lay dormant until "love is awakened" (Song of Solomon 8:4; make sure to read chapter 15, by the way!). There are many books and articles written that state that women have sexual desires but that they also appreciate nonsexual touches. There are so many nonsexual approaches that touch her soul, encouraging and highlighting her womanly ways. Being told she is alluring and difficult to forget throughout the day is just the beginning.

Putting effort into the message and expressing what it is about her that is alluring, what part of her body you can't get out of your mind, and what it means to know her heart belongs to you is the beginning to awakening love. Women often don't trust in a man's words because they believe there is something he expects behind every compliment. So, surprise her. Share your thoughts, put your strong arms around her, and let her know she is the true owner of your heart.

God has not only designed us to flourish in a relationship with Him, but He has intricately designed us to flourish in a relationship of oneness: emotionally, spiritually, physically, and even mentally. For her, oneness is the overflow that comes from long-lasting security, protection, and intimacy—a display of love so powerful it brings healing to her soul.

If you truly love her, enjoy her ways. Meet her desires. Awaken her love.

Ask Up!
Questions for Will and Way Conversations

1. What would you say women most desire in their marriage?

2. How do her desires differ from his? How are they similar?

3. What does it require for a man to truly and deeply discern the needs of a woman?

4. What do men need to understand about a woman's emotions and how to wisely approach them?

5. In what ways does a woman need *security* in her relationship with a man?

6. In what ways does a woman need *protection* in her relationship with a man?

7. In what ways does a woman need *intimacy* in her relationship with a man?

CHAPTER 14
Where There's a Will

You may not be able to change your spouse,
but you can change yourself.

—Gary Chapman

The Navy's Blue Angels aerial acrobatics performance is a sight to behold. As goodwill ambassadors and ace pilots, their very lives depend on working together as a team. Performing almost seventy airshows a year in front of over fifteen million people keeps these pilots on their toes. From flying their famous diamond formation to a host of other spectacular maneuvers, they must constantly be aware of one another and take painstaking care to fulfill their particular roles as precisely as possible.

The goal of the Blue Angels in their own words is simple—*"to look like one as they fly."* Doing so comes at a high price and involves weeks of practice and aerial choreography, knowledge of handling the machinery, and discipline of character to control the supersonic power, lightning-fast maneuverings, and speed capabilities of their vessels.

In each formation of the Blue Angels, one pilot leads and the others follow. One knows how to lead the way, and the others understand the importance of following. . .all for the purpose of being one. Yet, even as they follow someone, they are always leading someone else. In a sense, they are all leaders and followers. This requires constant communications, keeping one another always in sight, and extreme amounts of trust. It sounds much like a great marriage, doesn't it?

Every effort of these aerial acrobats, the Angels, has to be accurate. The element of surprise comes when the onlookers watch what they thought was one pattern split off into two, four, and more trails that weave out and then back in together. When asked how many times these stunts are accomplished perfectly, one Blue Angel leader said, "Out of one hundred times of performing, we only accomplish perfection five times—just enough to know that the challenge is attainable. But, we are always working at flying as one."[44]

Getting the will of a man and the way of a woman to fly together as one—now that is a sight to behold.

Flying Together

Whether you are a would-be Blue Angel pilot or a nervous newlywed, learning how to fly together with someone else and do it well is a process, and it takes time. Before the Blue Angels can fly well together, they must persevere through many days and months of practicing and of sometimes flying not quite so well together. What matters most is that they stay at it. Similarly, in the process of forging a meaningful marriage, when some difficulties arise, a husband or wife may start throwing in the towel far too soon.

For example, often when a man determines his will over a matter, his wife is concerned about the way he plans to carry it all out. The man often mistakes the woman's concerns as an out-and-out affront to his will. Within moments, his amygdala gets hijacked. His ego swells, and instead of *responding*, he *reacts*. Often he misreads her intentions and assumes something that just is not true. More often, her concern is not *her* will trumping *his* but rather that things are done in an appropriate way, a way that represents her and them as a couple well. We cannot express enough just how important this factor is to a woman.

Many men absolutely miss their golden opportunity in these instances. They mistake their wife's strong sense of direction and opinion as a threat to their ego. Instead of taking a complementary approach, they compete. Instead of treating it as a partnership, it becomes a battle. Perspective impacts passion. In other words, the way we *see* it determines the way we *feel* about it.

As the home wars ensue, many a man misses capitalizing on a wonderful gift—namely the gifts, skills, and graces of the woman God has given to him. If you are a man and you have kept reading this far, you may be saying by now, "Why does my wife have to be so strong in her opinions? Why can't she just do what I say?"

If you want to accomplish something great, you had better get used to being in the nest with other eagles. A woman of strong opinion who is valued and heard can be a man's greatest asset. Take it from a guy like me (Robert) who is married to an eagle (Pamela). Here is a principle that has helped me tremendously in understanding and navigating her strengths:

Principle:
The way of a woman was designed by God
not to be a *competitive threat*

but a *complementary crown*
to the man.

A virtuous and worthy wife
[earnest and strong in character] is
*the **crown** of **her husband.***

(Proverbs 12:4 AMPC)

For men with strong wives, viewing the strengths and gifts within the personality and heart of the woman in your life as a crown and not a threat is a big step in the process of balancing, bending, and blending as a couple. Rather than looking at her strengths as a threat to you, be reminded that you belong to each other. The truth is that if she shines, you shine. If she gets to move higher up the mountain, you get to go there with her. Remember, you are on this journey together. Her strength is not your competition; it is your crown. Wear it with pride and appreciation. It is God's gift to you.

Some men by now may be saying, "But how could I stoop to that level? How could you ask me to condescend in that way? It's humiliating to me as a man."

Stoop? What makes stooping something bad? It is actually quite a godly thing. As it turns out, not only god*ly* but God-like. The fact is that God stoops. Here's what David observed:

You protect me with your saving shield. You
support me with your right hand. You have
stooped to make me great.

(Psalm 18:35 NCV)

Flying Solo

The results of men trying to lead their families via their broken "compasses" in our culture has been devastating. Dysfunction and depression have grown up like weeds in what God intended to be flourishing gardens. As a result of Adam's sin, man was infected with what the Bible describes as a curse. God gave the bad news to Adam this way: "'Cursed is the ground because of you; through painful toil you will eat of it all the days of your life. It will produce thorns and thistles for you, and you will eat the plants of the field. By the sweat of your brow you will eat your food until you return to the ground, since from it you were taken; for dust you are and to dust you will return'" (Genesis 3:17–19 NIV).

Let's think about this. The curse of man was not work itself, but rather work "by the sweat of [the] brow." Adam had responsibilities in the garden *before* the fall. So work itself was not a bad thing. However, because of his sin, now a new difficulty would characterize his work. Considering this passage and the nature of man, I believe that this curse includes what I refer to as *a preoccupation with his ego and his occupation*. In other words, as a result of man's sin he now has a built-in tendency to wrap himself up, if not hide himself altogether, in his work. Work becomes his preoccupation; he becomes consumed with it, often overcommitted to it, and in a real sense, lost in it.

Is there any wonder Jesus asked, "'What good will it be for someone to gain the whole world, yet forfeit their soul?'" (Matthew 16:26 NIV). This tendency within a man has left many wives and children sorely lacking in the areas of intimacy and support in the home from the man of the house. While job performance ratings and profits for these men may have soared, homes have been hurt, souls have suffered, and do so to this day.

John Eldredge describes his struggle with this disengaged default mode this way:

> *Looking at marriage is something I don't do much, for the same reason I have been dodging the recent postcards from my dentist. ("Where have you been? You're overdue for a checkup!") I have come to realize that my posture toward my marriage is that posture of détente—a cordial peace accord in which we have both conceded a good deal of desire in exchange for smoother daily operations.*
>
> *It dawns on me that I related to my marriage like I relate to my health. I do the bare minimum to get by, hoping to get away with my indulgences and my neglect, throwing down some communication and a bit of romance now and then, like I take vitamins as a sort of insurance policy. I ignore my health, for the most part, and hope for the best.[45]*

Many men want deeply to discover how to effectively and appropriately care for their wives and children but often don't know where to begin. In many cases, at best, dads are men who live in the same houses as their wives and children do, but who fail to consistently engage them in any kind of meaningful, consistent relationship. Sadly, society is plastered with painful stories of deadbeat dads who've traded in a real family for some fleeting relationship, of fathers who abuse verbally and physically, and perhaps most prolific among them, of dads who are simply disinterested or disengaged.

THE DISENGAGED DAD

The disinterested or disengaged dad is vividly described by a true story from a famous young lady who had one. Erma Bombeck was a beloved and famous humorist who became well known for her popular column on family life. Although so many of her columns covered the lighter moments of home life, there was one in which she described a not-so-funny aspect of her upbringing, her relationship with her father. She noted that he did not focus on his fathering role and gave little to some of the things that matter most. His lack of engagement clearly remained a mystery to the late writer even into her final years. She wrote:

> One morning my father didn't get up and go to work. He went to the hospital and died the next day. I hadn't thought that much about him before. He was just someone who left and came home and seemed glad to see everyone. He opened the jar of pickles when no one else could. He was the only one in the house who wasn't afraid to go into the basement by himself. Whenever I played house, the mother doll had a lot to do. I never knew what to do with the daddy doll, so I had him say, "I'm going off to work now"; and I put him under the bed. The funeral was in our living room, and a lot of people came and brought all kinds of good

food and cakes. We never had so much company
before. I went to my room and felt under the
bed for the daddy doll, and when I found him,
I dusted him off and put him on my bed. He
never did anything. I didn't know his leaving
would hurt so much.

That little girl felt a gaping hole in her soul. It
was a pain and emptiness she could well remember
even as a middle-aged woman. Her daddy may
have thought he was providing for the family, but
he had missed something significant.[46]

For some children and wives, there is a man at home most every night, thank God, but it may seem that he is not really "with" them at all. (Notice the dad doll only said, "I'm going off to work now.") Oh sure, *physically* he is present. In the body, he is there, but within his soul, he has not yet arrived. Such a man may be too committed to his family to ever leave them physically or financially and yet be reluctant to genuinely open up his life and heart to them. Ironically, he may be spending every ounce of his energy providing the very things they, perhaps, need the very least. He may be an expert at fulfilling the family's financial commitments but not even in the starting blocks when it comes to nurturing and supporting their souls.

STRAIGHTEN UP AND FLY RIGHT
One of the most astounding, and controversial, ideas marriage therapists now suggest is that women are not the only

ones who should carry the "emotional labor" of making a marriage strong and fulfilling. Emotional labor represents "the work that goes into sustaining love, which usually falls to women."[47] As it turns out, a strong marriage needs a man to engage this area as well; in fact, research shows that a man's initiative in making a marriage work is the key determinant.

Gottman's research affirms this:

> *What men do in a relationship is, by a large margin, the crucial factor that separates a great relationship from a failed one. . . This doesn't mean that a woman doesn't do her part, but the data proves that a man's actions are the key variable that determines whether a relationship succeeds or fails.*[48]

Joshua stands out among the husbands and fathers of scripture in particular as a man who had an engaged will devoted to God. His unflinching commitment to his family and to his nation paints a compelling picture of what goes into building a home where God is honored. It is a great example of the right uses of a man's will. Who wouldn't want to "fly" in a plane piloted by him?

Considering the hardships Joshua endured and the fact that he held to his faith and his principles right up to his death, I am interested and intrigued to take a closer look at the soul of this man. What was it on the interior of Joshua's life that gave him the strength and resolve to face the exterior challenges that so often surrounded him?

The deathbed statement of the man who was summoned by the Spirit to fill Moses' shoes is classic: "'But as for me and my household, we will serve the LORD'" (Joshua 24:15 NIV).

Joshua was not only called to lead the nation of Israel into the enemy-infested Promised Land, but it is clear that he was also called, first and foremost, to lead his family flock in the direction of God's will—to "pilot" that plane well. Some in today's world would label his proclamation as "stubborn," "narrow-minded," or "chauvinistic." On the contrary, I'd call it "assertive," "intentional," and "purposeful." In fact, we think Joshua is the kind of man many young women are hoping and praying for.

What intrigues us the most about Joshua as a family man is his vision and conviction. Purpose and passion filled the words and actions of this father and husband. Not only did he have a clear understanding of where he needed to lead his family and how, but Joshua also had the strength of will to do so. Such an engaged will, I believe, was drawn out of Joshua through the conflicts and challenges he endured. Wrapped up within this one determined statement are *four solid bricks that build a home* that had their foundation within the soul of this man.

Your will is *set*: In his statement of *a man's determination*, the first thing I see is *a man's commitment to God* ("As for me"). Before Joshua could possibly speak for his wife and children, he first had to speak for himself and his own commitment to God.

For a man to propose to lead his family in following Christ collectively, he must first make the decision to follow Him personally. Joshua could confidently say, "As for me. . ." because he had committed himself to pursuing his own relationship with God. Even as a young aide to Moses,

Joshua would linger in the place of prayer long after Moses had returned to camp (Exodus 33:11). The determination of a man's will to lead a family God's way can only be sustained when it flows honestly, right from a man's soul. The man who authentically loves and knows God will want his wife and children to know the same.

In order to lead a family or marriage, a man needs to know how to lead himself. Timothy Keller cites a professor of history who wrote that "for most of Western history, the primary and most-valued characteristic of manhood was self-mastery. . . . A man who indulged in excessive eating, drinking, sleeping or sex—who failed to 'rule himself'—was considered unfit to rule his household."[49] As Proverbs says, "He who. . .rules his spirit [is better] than he who captures a city" (Proverbs 16:32 NASB).

Your will is *shared*: Second (brick 2) is *a man's vision for his family* ("and my house, we…"). When you were a child, perhaps like many other children you were asked the question, "What do you want to be when you grow up?" Now that you are an adult, maybe the questions have changed to "What do you want to do when you retire?" or "Where would you like to travel?" But has anyone ever asked you, "What do you want your kids to be like when they grow up?" "What kind of people do you hope they will be?" "What kind of souls do you hope they will have?" Joshua's sense of responsibility obviously went well beyond the management of his own personal schedule, finances, and behavior. He had a vision and that vision included his wife and children.

Too often today, in the name of entrepreneurship, men are incited to grasp after visions that include everything but

what should be considered a man's most priceless investments, his wife and kids. The "successful" man is often considered to be the one who has the biggest house, the most
expensive car, the biggest bank account, the biggest title, etc.
The hottest-selling magazine titles reveal much about our
priorities (i.e., *Fortune, Money, Self, Success*, etc.).

On the contrary and running against the grain of culture,
the only "biggest" that the God of the Bible is impressed
with in a man's life is bigness of soul. Although he was
ultimately responsible for all of Israel and, before God, was
the "head honcho" of such, Joshua was stout-hearted enough
to approach his vision not only in his own name but in the
name of his family as well. What touched them touched him.
What he pursued, he pursued not only for them but *along
with* them, as well.

Your will is *solid*: Third (brick 3), is *a man's motivation*
("will"). This part strikes a nerve within me that pulsates in
the form of a few questions. They go something like this:
Since when did we decide that children know what's best
for their lives? When did we stop leading and compelling
our families to do the right thing? What ever happened to
"Father knows best"?

No, I am *not* advocating a tyrannical emergence of male
dominance. However, I *am* asserting the fact that men of
God must become effective at asserting themselves as leaders.
There *is* a time when a man must draw the line and say to
his child, "No, you are not going to that party because I am
not comfortable with the fact that no chaperones will be
present." There *is* a time when a man must put his foot down
and say to his family, "We are turning this television off or

changing the channel. I will not allow this kind of language or these images to fill our home."There *is* a time when a man must begin to take a proactive posture spiritually rather than one that is compromisingly *re*active.

Joshua was proactive in his spiritual leadership. With a made-up mind, he had a clear vision of what his family should be and was determined to take every step he could to ensure that it would become all that it was meant to be. He did not hesitate to assert his influence and his energy toward that end. In Joshua's world, hesitation would have meant death. You see, it was Joshua who was selected to lead Israel out of the desert into the Promised Land (Joshua 3:1–17). It was Joshua who was called to unify the people of God (Joshua 1:10–18). It was Joshua who was called to help the people conquer the Canaanites, the pesky enemies who wanted to destroy Israel (Joshua 10–12). It was Joshua who had the responsibility of dividing the land up among the people (Joshua 13–19).

The best definition for the role of a leader I have ever heard came from Dr. Robert Cooley, a seminary president and archaeologist. He said, "A leader is someone who does two things: He frames issues and engages conflict."[50] At his best, a leader not only recognizes the issues he and those around him are facing, but he helps others to see them as well.

Recognizing needs, however, is just half the battle. What makes a man a leader is his willingness to engage the conflicts in his life, in his home, in his work, in his church with love, with patience, with vision, and with confidence.

Every man is beckoned by the Spirit of God, and the

truth of scripture is to be proactive in his leadership. You and I need every ounce of influence and energy we can find to lead our families closer to God. After all, we have been selected to lead our children from their desert experiences of adolescence into the hoped-for land of adulthood; no one else has been appointed by God to do that. We bear the duty of working to unify our families, of helping our wife and kids overcome the enemies that would strike at their souls, and to, ultimately, divide and share the wisdom and provisions that come from God's hand with them.

Your will is *surrendered*—Finally, the fourth (brick 4) essential in Joshua's example is *a man's mission* ("serve the Lord"). This essential was the absolute focal point of Joshua's life as a man, as a military leader, as a husband, and as a father. This speaks so clearly of the passion that fueled this man's life. He was riveted on the goal of serving the purposes of God in his life. Whether it was another Canaanite city to overthrow or an unseemly characteristic in one of his children to correct, Joshua was centered upon serving God. Ordinary people accomplish extraordinary things by focusing their lives. Whether it involved leading a nation across a river and into an unknown land or leading his wife to a place of prayer, Joshua saw it as one thing and one thing alone—serving the Lord. Joshua had learned the secret of living life one way—a surrendered will, from the soul and before an audience of One.

ASK UP!
Questions for Will and Way Conversations

1. Have you ever watched the aerial acrobatics of the Navy's Blue Angels or the Air Force's Thunderbirds? From the start, what would you imagine are some of the things that have to go into preparing for these choreographed marvels?

2. What does it take for the will of a man and the way of a woman to "fly" together well in life?

3. What happens when we tend to fly "solo" in our marriages? How does it affect us and our home?

4. What does the will of a man at its best bring to a marriage and to a family?

5. In what ways do men tend to overuse or abuse the influence of their will?

6. If men pull back in their roles and responsibilities in the home, how does it affect their wives and children?

7. In what ways did Joshua exemplify the will of a man at its best?

8. What will it take for you to surrender your will more fully to God at this season in your life?

CHAPTER 15
The Will and the Way. . .
in the Bedroom

To be fully seen by somebody, then, and be loved
anyhow—this is a human offering that can
border on miraculous.

—Elizabeth Gilbert

Nakedness is compelling. In the garden of Eden, Adam and Eve were "naked and unashamed" (Genesis 2:25). The environment must have been heaven on earth. A man. A woman. A garden full of nourishment. A God watching over them both. Protected. Safe. Free. No clothing necessary.

To Adam and Eve it wasn't seen as "nakedness"; it was normalcy. Their sinless environment and natures permitted them to share in absolute openness. After all, they had nothing to prove, nothing to fear, and nothing to hide. They were altogether free, in the truest sense, to look upon each other in all their glory. They could be themselves completely and without apology. No inhibitions. No comparisons. A fearless atmosphere. Completely secure. Free to be what God had intended.

THE FIRST LOOK
When Adam first gazed upon the magnetic beauty of his unadorned bride, his words said it all: "'This is now bone of

my bones and flesh of my flesh; she shall be called 'woman,' for she was taken out of man'" (Genesis 2:23 NIV). He set the goal, "You are a part of me, and I am a part of you. We exist to be united, to share deeply, to be one."

The passage continues: "Therefore shall a man leave his father and his mother, and shall cleave unto his wife: and they shall be one flesh. And they were both naked, the man and his wife, and were not ashamed" (Genesis 2:24–25 KJV). From the start, men and women were compelled toward each other, toward what we describe as oneness. They were drawn. The pull was magnetic and intrinsic.

Naked and unashamed. Perhaps these two adjectives describe best the intimacy that a man and wife can share within the "marriage bed" (Hebrews 13:4), which the scripture describes as an honorable place that is clean, undefiled. The New Testament paints a picture of this place as being the closest thing to Eden men and women may know in this life. A man and his wife, enveloped in each other. Open. Uninhibited. Abandoned. Selfless. Unburdened. The place, the privilege, and the idea were all a part of God's masterful design. He had it all in mind before we ever did. A relationship toward Eden rediscovered.

INTIMACY THREATENED

When sin entered the garden, innocence left. As a matter of fact, the passage seems to suggest that just after the couple ate the forbidden fruit that their next step told it all. They soon "made coverings for themselves" (Genesis 3:7 NIV)—the text implies that Adam made his own and Eve hers. Instead of living to serve God and each other, they suddenly became all too aware of themselves.

Enter selfishness.

When sin entered the garden, the first thing Adam and Eve were aware of was their own nakedness: "Then the eyes of both of them were opened, and they realized they were naked" (Genesis 3:7 NKJV). It is interesting to observe here what the scripture does not say. It does not say, "Their eyes were opened. . .and they became aware of their guilt." It does not say, "Their eyes were opened. . .and they became aware of their sin." It does not say, "Their eyes were opened. . .and they became aware of the crime they committed." It says, "Their eyes were opened. . .and they became aware of their nakedness." Apparently, they did not become *sin*-aware, but rather *self*-aware.

Exit intimacy.

And then, the couple "heard the sound of the Lord God as he was walking in the garden in the cool of the day, and they hid from the Lord God among the trees of the garden" (Genesis 3:8 NIV). Ironic, isn't it? God's created beings trying to hide from their Creator amid His creation.

And then God asked that haunting question that resounds through the ages: "'Where are you?'" (v. 9 NIV).

Adam's response reveals the struggle of his own soul: "'I heard you in the garden, and I was afraid because I was naked; so I hid'" (v. 10 NIV).

God's response searched the soul of this man more deeply: "'Who told you that you were naked? Have you eaten from the tree that I commanded you not to eat from?'" (v. 11 NIV).

Interesting, isn't it? Adam is riveted on the results of the tragedy—"I am afraid" and "I am exposed." All the while, God gets to the source of the dilemma—"Did you do what I instructed you *not* to do?" Once again, God speaks the truth and man finds himself running from it. How many times has that happened in diverse ways since that dreadful day? In what ways are we doing that this very moment? And oh, the intimacies with God and with spouse that have been forfeited along the way.

In that tragic moment of compromise, the first man and woman lost their sense of identity. Instead of protecting each other, they began to accuse each other. Rather than sharing, they withdrew. In that moment, man not only lost right standing with God, he lost a right relationship with his wife. A chasm developed that has carried on to every culture and every marriage, even yours. A gulf between them emerged. A bridge back to Eden was desperately needed.

Yet, to this day, nakedness is compelling. A man has a deep inner longing to look upon and to hold his wife unclothed, uninhibited, and utterly abandoned to him. And, while certainly a wife often desires physical closeness and intimacy with her husband, in a unique way a woman also often has a deeper inner craving to look upon and to touch her husband's soul, uncovered, uninhibited, and utterly abandoned and open to herself.

A naked body.

A naked soul.

A compelling desire for intimacies.

A longing for Eden again.

By this we do not mean to imply that a man does not

desire to be close to his wife spiritually or a wife to her husband physically. On the contrary, those desires exist, although they are not always perceived as primary. Perhaps this explains why, men seek out counseling often because of sexual frustrations and women because of interpersonal frustrations.

A MAN'S STRENGTH AND A WOMAN'S BEAUTY

John and Stasi Eldredge convey the differences that emerge when a man and woman make love. Admittedly, they qualify their vivid description as "a delicate analogy." As you read this, consider the will and the way aspects of lovemaking and the differences men and women bring to the experience.

> *When they are making love, the man penetrates his woman as he offers his strength. The woman invites the man into herself. If the man will not rise to the occasion, there will be no intercourse, no fireworks. He must move; his strength must come forth before he can enter her. If he is passive, it will not happen. But neither will the love consummate unless the woman opens herself to him. If she is guarded, no union will take place. The man enters his woman and offers her his strength; she draws him in, embraces and envelopes him. And that is how life is created.[51]*

Uniquely, the will of a man and the way of a woman bring different but complementary offerings to their sexual intimacy. The will of a man desires a place to convey his strength. This goes beyond an act of power or simply sex; it frees his soul to abandon himself to expressing his love for his wife, his lover, through his strength. The places of sexual intimacy, if but for a few glorious moments, allow a man to live his life from his soul and express aspects of the image of God, the *Imago Dei*, given to man through engagement and initiative.

In similar manner, through sexual union and expression, the woman finds freedom to express aspects of the image of God entrusted to her through her grace and beauty. She comes alive with allure, tenderness, and abandonment to deep expressions of love. She chooses to give and to welcome love in the depths of her body and soul. She who was drawn out of man welcomes him back into herself.

But the engagements of intimacy start long before a couple enters the bedroom. They come in the rhythmic and sensitive responses to each other's needs and souls before they engage in the acts of lovemaking. Sexual intercourse is preceded by emotional awareness and tender discourse. It occurs when he becomes aware of her, her presence, her need of his encouragement, his companionship, his touch. It is kindled when she intentionally acts on what she understands his needs are, her awareness engaging a moment of acceptance.

Love is awakened in a thousand different ways. The man sees something about the woman's ways and her beauty that alone can tap the springs of his masculinity and loving strength. Something about his tender strength and faithful kindnesses can draw out her softer sides, her deep passions, and make her feel beautiful again. It begins every time he steps up his interest in her and every time she lets down her guard with him.

The roles of husband and wife are not just titles on a certificate; they are assignments that call for married people to fill them. *When men pull back* and become passive in the relationship, they diminish the image of God in them and starve their wives emotionally. But something else also happens. We have seen it too many times. While women desire to exhibit their strengths, no wife wants to have to fill her role *and* his in a marriage or relationship. But when men pull back from loving leadership in their homes, they create a vacuum, one that must be filled by someone. When men pull back, women power up.

When women power up in the marriage due to a need the husband is not filling, it undermines something of their God-given essence, influence, and strength. Ultimately, the woman resents the man for "leaving" her to carry the weight of his physical, emotional, or spiritual absence. She is left to herself to find protection, provision for her own soul, endeavoring to survive isolation, much like a woman who was left alone in front of the Tree of Good and Evil. A woman, desperate to survive aloneness, has the potential to unknowingly emasculate her husband's spirit, stealing away the strength that was intended to produce life.

THE PORCUPINE PRINCIPLE

Few people in the world have studied marriage and the marriage relationship from an empirical standpoint more than Dr. John Gottman. In some of his early studies, he was required to watch films of almost every animal known to man having sex. He watched elephants, horses, dogs, camels, giraffes, mice, zebras, tigers, lions, bears, you name it—he saw it, all of them caught in the act. After viewing these, he had three main observations: (1) "these acts were amazingly fast"; (2) "none of the animals looked like they were having a whole lot of fun"—(3) except for the porcupine![52]

First of all, one would imagine that something that looked like a porcupine would be incapable of sex. The quills alone would pose a problem. They are completely covered with them. The male porcupine faces a unique challenge. He wants to have sex with his female counterpart, but if he approaches her too quickly, and her quills are up, he is going to get terribly hurt, even injured. What he does next is quite amazing.

The male porcupine simply sits down and faces the female. Then, he carefully places his paws on the sides of her face and strokes it very slowly and gently. He does this over and over again, patiently it seems. After a while, he goes behind her to see if her quills have settled down. If not, he resumes his former place in front of her and continues to stroke her face. How long does he do this? For as long as it takes. Once her quills are down, the sex can proceed without injury to either of them.

When it comes to sexuality, perhaps the porcupine understands the secret of the will and the way better than other animals, and better than some humans for that matter. You could say that instead of simply asserting sexual "will," the male somehow understands and attends to the "way" needed by the female for intimacy to occur. Guys could take some cues from Mr. Porcupine. In fact, Gottman's research "found that men who learned emotional attunement got what they ultimately wanted from their relationships: less fighting and more sex."[53]

A little bit of understanding, and sometimes a bit of tender stroking, can go a long way. Gottman adds this advice:

> *Passion begins in the mind. When a woman feels passionate—whether it's about her work, her family, or you—her body comes alive, her emotions are heightened, and she is capable of experiencing an incredible amount of pleasure and having amazing sensual experiences. But this capacity for ecstasy always begins in a woman's mind and heart. They are her most powerful erogenous zones.*
>
> *To truly know a woman's body you have to first know her mind and heart. . . . A woman needs to feel connected to feel desire. She needs to feel emotionally and physically safe with you before she can feel completely safe sexually.*[54]

STARVING FOR IT

Many wives and husbands today are starving for more intimacy in their lives, in their marriages. Intimacy is realized when sufficient trust and openness occur within a relationship so that one individual can express his or her inner needs, hurts, dreams, and desires to another comfortably and confidently. When the atmosphere in a relationship is constructed that lends itself to that kind of expression, it does more than merely warm a marriage. Something greater occurs. Souls connect. Two lives have a chance to unite and blend.

Intimacy cannot be forced out, driven out, or demanded. No remote control exists that, upon command, can cause the thoughts, concerns, feelings, and longings of a spouse's soul to suddenly appear. Intimacy is something that must be *drawn* out in a relationship, summoned. Proverbs 20:5 (NIV) says, "The purposes of a person's heart are deep waters, but one who has insight draws them out."

Intimacy comes from the Latin *intimus*, meaning "in most." Men and women both need intimacy; they need to feel connected. Gottman says that "women need to feel emotionally connected to have sex, and men need to have sex in order to feel emotionally connected."[55] Coming to understand each other, to see through each other's lenses, can bring the grace and truth into the bedroom needed to enjoy more oneness physically.

NAKED AND UNASHAMED

There are two places God has provided for us to be "naked" and "unashamed"—two places we can go. The first place we can go and bare our souls without hesitation or reservation is into the presence of God together. When we pray, we can tell Him everything, unload everything, for He knows better than anyone else.

David was comfortable standing soul-bare and open in the presence of God. Consider his words:

> *You have searched me, LORD, and you know me.*
> *You know when I sit and when I rise; you per-*
> *ceive my thoughts from afar. . .you are familiar*
> *with all my ways. . . . Where can I go from your*

Spirit? Where can I flee from your presence? If I go up to the heavens, you are there; if I make my bed in the depths, you are there. If I rise on the wings of the dawn, if I settle on the far side of the sea, even there your hand will guide me, your right hand will hold me fast.

(Psalm 139:1–3, 7–10 NIV)

The writer of Hebrews painted a vivid picture of how a man stands before the presence and Word of God:

No creature is hidden from Him, but all things are naked and exposed to the eyes of Him to whom we must give an account.

(Hebrews 4:13 HCSB)

The second place we can go to be naked and unashamed is our marriage relationship. There is no place in which I can be myself more freely and completely than when I am at home, in the embrace of my wife, my lover. At home, I don't have to act, perform, pretend, or strive.

No one knows me as well as my wife. My strengths, my struggles, my values, my doubts, my sins, my accomplishments, my longings, my fears, my hopes, my failures, and my dreams. She knows all about them. I have become exposed to her and she to me. The veil has been removed. . .and it continues to be, more and more. And amazingly, she still loves me. . .as I never dreamt I could be loved.

Ask Up!
Questions for Will and Way Conversations

(NOTE: Since the questions for this chapter are more intimate and private in nature, they are offered as suggestions for married couples to ask each other within the context of their marriage.)

How close are you to your spouse? How comfortable are you unclothed. . .physically and spiritually? Here are some questions you can use to carefully approach these sensitive, and yet significant, areas of your marriage partnership:

1. Why is human nature so preoccupied with nakedness? What is the reason for it?

2. To ask one another: How did you feel on our wedding day after the wedding when we were en route to our room for the night? What was going through your mind and heart as you anticipated the consummation of our marriage? Be honest.

3. What was it like for you the first time you saw me naked? How did you feel when you first disrobed in front of me? What thoughts were coursing through your mind? Where do you think they came from?

4. In what way is nakedness an important part of closeness in our marriage? How would it be different if it was not a part of our relationship?

5. Have I been as quick to expose my soul to you as I have my body? How can you tell?

6. When have our souls felt the closest as a couple?

7. Describe a time when you felt I really opened my soul to you. How did it affect our relationship? How did my doing that make you feel?

8. What is sexual intimacy like for you when our souls are distant?

9. What is sexual intimacy like for you when our souls are close? Is there a connection between spiritual intimacy and sexual intimacy in our relationship? Explain.

10. What could I do to make you more comfortable being physically or spiritually close to me?

CHAPTER 16
Restoring Marriage:
Living God's Will, God's Way

You come to love not by finding the perfect person, but by seeing an imperfect person perfectly.
—Sam Keen

What is the most "beautiful" word in the English language? Do you know? What would you say it is? What would your spouse say?

Recently, *Reader's Digest* asked their subscribers to complete the sentence, "The most beautiful sound in the world is. . ." One of them was a mom who added in the comments, "The sound of my sons saying 'Mom, I'm home!'"[56]

That was it. Many would agree, yet many would beg to differ. Regardless of your former experience, just what *does* it take to make a house into a "home"?

Proverbs gives us this blueprint:

> *By wisdom a house is built, and by understanding it is established; and by knowledge the rooms are filled with all precious and pleasant riches.*
> (Proverbs 24:3–4 NASB)

Most Christians would agree that the only way to make a house into a home is to fill it with more of Christ. In order to fill the world with His presence and glory, God created a man and then created a woman out of the man. In a glorious reflection of the Trinitarian union, God formed the first couple, the first marriage, and the first home. Not only were they the beginning, in some sense, they are the blueprint.

The will and the way in marriage is a reflection of something even greater than the relationship itself. Along our journey of married life, we have come to see and believe that in creation God has entrusted some aspects of His image to man and others to woman. They are complementary stewards of the image of God—the *Imago Dei*. Marriage represents a merging of these two complementary natures.

Marriages, then, are Trinitarian reflections. Also, they embody two aspects of God's nature that remind us of two important things—that is, of God's will and of God's way. Marriage is an earthly relationship designed to reflect a heavenly one. Paul paints that picture quite clearly in his letter to the Ephesians (chapter 5). He describes the way in which husbands and wives can relate to one another in order to recover something of the oneness of Eden in their relationship. But he also paints an analogous backdrop of Christ the Bridegroom and the Church, His bride.

We believe the foundation of every relationship in life, especially marriage, is our own relationship with God through His Son Jesus Christ. While you work on your marriage, make sure you don't miss out on growing in knowing God and walking with Him each day. Put your full faith and trust in God. You will find the closer you draw to Him, the closer He will draw to you.

God also wants to restore marriages today, and so many of them need restoring. He can do this in our nation, and He can do it in your life, powerfully. Remember, when God wanted to bring salvation to the world, He did not introduce His Son as *a leader* to a nation, but rather as *a son to a family.* The Trinity loves the family and honors it, because in a sense the Trinity is a family of persons.

It is important, however, to remember and recover the glorious purpose of marriage.

The *Oxford Dictionary* gives us two brief definitions of the word *marriage*:

1. The legally or formally recognized union of a man and a woman as partners in a relationship; and,

2. A combination or mixture of two or more elements.

So, while the first definition may be expected, the second one adds yet another dimension. As it turns out, the word *marriage* represents not just a relational or covenantal state of being, but (as definition 2 states) it is a process of blending, forging, and combining two "elements" together. In the case of marriage, that involves nothing less than the will of a man and the way of a woman.

God designed marriage from the beginning in order to not only fill the earth with people, but also to fill it with His glory. The millions and millions of "little" marriage circles drawn all over the planet are designed to reflect the "greater" marriage circle of the Church's relationship as a bride with Jesus," the Bridegroom. "For the earth will be filled with the knowledge of the glory of the Lord as the waters cover the sea" (Habakkuk 2:14 NIV).

Why Marriage?

There are at least seven reasons why God made marriage that we see and believe need to be reemphasized today in every way possible. It is worth working to restore and nurture it in our churches, communities, and nation and in the hearts and minds of emerging generations. These reasons are deeply rooted in theology but also consistently confirmed in research—including the monumental work accomplished by the Gottmans and others.

The question is worth considering, and someone should write the book on it: *How would our world be different if the value and place of marriage had diminished in our world one hundred years ago or one thousand?* God has used marriage in untold ways as the birthing, nurturing, and launching context for humanity. God created marriage for so many reasons, which include:

Reason 1—Because loneliness is so bad. At some point after God created the first male, Adam, He looked at him in his setting and made an observation that evaluated the man in that moment. Here is what he said, "It is not good that the man should be alone" (Genesis 2:18 KJV). While aspects of Adam's behavior, mood, or disposition surely reflected this, it is an ongoing sight to see all around us. God first spotted loneliness in Adam, the individual, and He did something about it. He filled the need. The remedy He chose was to make or draw someone "out of" Adam. In a sense, before God ever said "these two shall become one" through marriage, when God first made Eve, it was something more along the lines of *this one shall become two.*

Reason 2—Because unity is so good. In fact, unity is a reflection of God Himself. In the Old Testament, the psalmist described God's view of authentic community: "How good and pleasant it is when God's people live together in unity! . . . For there the LORD bestows his blessing, even life forevermore" (Psalm 133:1, 3 NIV). Did you catch the promise? Imagine the opportunity to be in a place where God "commands" His blessing. That is a family. In the Gospels, Jesus described such not-to-be-missed moments as the places He would show up: "Where two or three are gathered together in my name, there am I in the midst of them" (Matthew 18:20 KJV).

Reason 3—Because selfishness will shrink your world. As we discussed in the last chapter, once Adam and Eve became aware of their sin and shame, the first thing they did was to "[make] coverings for themselves" (Genesis 3:7 NIV). The language used here would imply that instead of serving each other they became more aware of themselves, not in an insightful way but rather more of a paranoid one. Not only did shame enter the garden and their hearts, but so did fear, and fear is the opposite of love. From that moment they moved into efforts to justify their sin, and, instead of quickly repenting, they began to offer accusations of others deemed more responsible than they in their failure. Selfishness diminishes our view and our souls.

Reason 4—Because sharing will enlarge your world. Chuck Swindoll has said, "We are never more like God than when we are giving."[57] Marriage provides a 24-7 context for men and women to practice loving, giving, and sharing in so many ways. Through marriage every day you and I can "serve one another humbly in love" (Galatians 5:13 NIV), "deny [ourselves]" (Matthew 16:24 NIV), put each other's interests before our own (Philippians 2:4), "humble [ourselves]" (1 Peter 5:6 NIV), submit [ourselves] one to another (Ephesians 5:21), and lay down our lives for a friend (John 15:13). Counterintuitively, when we share or give of ourselves, we don't shrink or diminish. On the contrary, we emerge, expand, and enlarge. "Give, and it shall be given unto you" (Luke 6:38 KJV).

Reason 5—Because a marriage can reflect the glory of God. Marriage is the first context God made in which man could experience and practice unity and community. Ultimately, marriage is a reflection of the divine community, the Trinity. While some would assume that the "image of God" can best be viewed by an individual looking in a mirror, it would be more biblical to say it can be seen in unity, in community—not in a mirror, but more so in a marriage. Pamela would say a good marriage needs more windows than mirrors. In fact, the Bible begins with a "marriage" (Genesis 1 and 2) with the union of Adam and Eve, and it ends with the "marriage supper of the Lamb" (Revelation 19:6–9), when Jesus and His bride are reunited in heaven. The Bible is a marriage book.

Reason 6—Because a marriage can produce godly sons and daughters. This purpose for marriage in the Bible can easily be passed over. In the space of a few words, the Bible tells us one of the great reasons for marriage—"Didn't the LORD make you one with your wife? In body and spirit you are his. And what does he want? Godly children from your union. So guard your heart; remain loyal to the wife of your youth" (Malachi 2:15 NLT).

Reason 7—Because a marriage can reveal the heart of God and His love for us as can nothing else. In Ephesians 5, the apostle Paul describes roles for husbands and wives in marriage. It appears his purpose is to help them rediscover some of the relational connection and motivation originally intended for the garden of Eden. His description is two-dimensional, although some have tried to interpret it rigidly. In the sweeping context of Paul's writings, he doesn't endorse autocratic approaches to family life or church life but rather urges attitudes of humility, service, and honor. Again, Paul draws the reader of Ephesians to ponder the great analogous nature of marriage as the "profound mystery" that it is. In fact, he uses it to describe the relationship of Christ and His church. Marriage is not only an opportunity, a relationship—it is a revelation of glorious relationship available to men and women and ultimately expressed in the joyous union that is the Trinity.

THE SOUL KEEPER

I (Pamela) love anything romantic, and I've learned to appreciate how some of the simplest moments of life can be simply romantic. It doesn't always require candlelight and flowers, music doesn't *have* to be playing (though it really helps!); it doesn't always have to include gift bags and wrapped boxes. Romance is something that begins to take place when the world stands still, and if but for a short while, it feels like you're the only two people there. No comparisons and no competition, no words, just the two of you together.

One warm July evening, beneath some very bright stars, Robert and I stood on a Virginian hillside. It felt like just the two of us, but actually we were surrounded by hundreds and hundreds of youth at a Jesus festival. Serving as youth pastors at the time, our life seemed full of responsibilities. This particular evening was the closing session to what had been a great week with our New York youth at the weeklong event, and we were getting ready to share communion outside on a hillside under the stars.

I still have vivid memories of that evening, the feelings of closeness and spiritual oneness as Robert and I stood, communion cup in one hand and holding hands with the other, outside under the stars. Often when I am outside, I feel as if I am in God's sanctuary and preparing for communion. Outside on a hillside under the stars that summer was no different. Everything seemed more energized with what felt like the Lord's presence. I remember thinking, *Wow, this is so amazing!* Beautiful worship music, standing near each other, eyes closed, and fully engaged in the moment, all while holding hands outside on a hillside under the stars. There was romance in the air. What is it that occurs for us girls? These spiritual moments create these emotional highs, and life feels so perfect. Couldn't life just stand still?

I was wholeheartedly thanking the Lord for our wonderful relationship and marriage, thanking the Lord for blessing me with such a handsome and sexy husband (is that spiritual? I hope so!), and holding on even tighter when I heard this quiet but familiar Fatherly voice say, *"Let go of his hand."*

That couldn't be God's voice. He wants us to be "one" as a couple, right?

Again this quiet voice inside said, *"Let go of his hand."*

My romantic thoughts and emotions were jerked back into reality, and I thought, *Why would I want to do that?*

Just obey. "Let go of his hand."

As I slowly let go of Robert's hand, I took a step to the side to put a bit more space between us and thought, *Okay, what now?* I'll never forget what came next. The Spirit of the Lord impressed my heart with these words: *"There will be a day you will stand in front of Me, not as Robert Crosby's wife, but as My daughter. You will stand on your own. The relationship I desire to have with you cannot be achieved on your husband's prayer time, but you must come to Me on your own time."* It was as if the romantic atmosphere was cracked through, and a spotlight opened up over my head, getting me ready for some "soul" surgery.

At that time in our marriage, I admit I was often the "dripping faucet" complaining about our lack of devotional time together. I would often say to Robert, "How can I grow spiritually if you don't take more time to pray with me?" I thought the best of life was to be shared, and it included prayer together, growing together spiritually, and embracing the adventure of God's Word.

While there is a lot to be said about the responsibility of spiritual formation as a couple, this should not be to the neglect of caring for your own soul and relationship with the Lord. No one can be the keeper of your soul like you can as you "[build] your[self] up in your most holy faith" (Jude 1:20 NIV). In fact, it isn't anyone else's responsibility but yours and mine to develop the level of relationship that the Spirit of God invites us into. And it is so much sweeter to know that the Lord will lead you and speak to you directly. He desires to grow your soul and uncover treasures in His Word that will transform your perspective, your longings, and your understanding.

Getting back to the Mary and Joseph story, remember that God did not bring the news of the annunciation, of the coming birth of Jesus, to them together as a couple. Certainly, He could have done so. It could have come in the form of premarital counseling, but it did not. Rather, God chose to call out their obedience and surrender to His will and His plan individually. In separate moments, He called out the will of a man and also drew out the way of a woman, uniting them to do His will His way.

Start It Up!

When a marriage is going through tough times, when a couple has grown distant or resentful toward each other—which one should take the first step toward healing and restoration? Traditionally, and arguably from the Ephesians 5 chapter, it should be the husband. But honestly either the husband or the wife could, and should, do so. Why?

Taking the first step toward forgiveness, healing, and restoration in marriage is Christlike—that is why. We are so glad that Jesus did not wait for the world to "get its act together" or "straighten up" or "change its attitude" before He moved in our direction. The New Testament tells us "*While we were still sinners*, Christ died for us" (Romans 5:8 NIV, emphasis added). He took the first step toward us before we had our act together, "while we were still sinners." Loving husbands and wives are wise to do the same.

No matter how frustrated or disappointed you may be right now with the person you love, there is a sure place you can begin to rebuild—or to truly build for the first time—a meaningful and love-lasting relationship. There is a place to start or to begin again. The will and the way can walk hand in hand, even soul to soul, if they can remember and apply this.

If you are a woman, continue to study your man and discover how best to speak to his will. Put extra effort into *respecting* his will and still *expressing* your way. In other words, remember as you speak to your man that although his will may sometimes seem quite strong, matters of the will matter much to him. Make sure you don't stop expressing your true feelings, even if it is sometimes awkward. Remember, you can respect his will without sacrificing your convictions.

And if you are a man, determine to *express* your will and yet to *respect* her way all the while. Since feeling a strong sense of security and partnership in her relationship with you is so important, don't handle her like a bull in a china shop. Hold her carefully, gently, and lovingly. Your effectiveness as a loving leader is not expressed in how forceful you are but ultimately in how effective you are in guiding her to follow God's plan together with you.

There You Are

Last, someone has said there are two kinds of people in the world, and you can tell by the way they walk into a room.

One rushes into the room full of themselves and says, "Here I am." We all know people like that, don't we?

Then there are others who walk in and instead say, "There *you* are." These people are riveted in their focus on others. This struck a chord the first time we heard it. You can see such people filling these roles in families and churches every day. Once we shared this idea with another leader, he responded with this: "I like that comparison you made. I really believe there are people who will do just that. But what about this: While there is the person who walks in the room and says, 'Here I am', and another that says, 'There you are' . . .how about the person who says, 'Here *we* are'?"

That's it. That is unity and community. It is what God wants to bring into your marriage since it represents who He is. It's the *balance* of the will and the way acknowledged by two souls learning to *bend* toward one another, to work together. It is all about doing God's will God's way in marriage and in life. It is the beauty of the *blend* only God can bring when "two become one" and you choose every day to journey together toward a true oneness.

ASK UP!

Questions for Will and Way Conversations

1. What are some other words that you think are truly beautiful?

2. In what ways does a good marriage reflect the Trinity?

3. Why do you think God chose to cover the planet with marriages and family "circles"? What purpose was there in this approach to filling the earth?

4. What was a time when you felt truly lonely? How did it affect you and your life overall? How did you pull out of it?

5. Is marriage at risk in our world today? Is it losing ground or gaining ground? How so?

6. What is the purpose of marriage?

7. What can we do to see marriage redeemed and restored to what God originally intended?

ACKNOWLEDGMENTS

Thank you (from Robert) to Pamela, the love of my life, that young lady I met in the college library one evening when I answered her first question that was all about a word, just one word. If you remember, I actually ended up answering it *without a word*. Thank you for allowing me to share in the adventures and conversations of your life ever since! I love you. . .for all time.

Thank you (from Pamela) to Robert, the one who still makes my heart melt. Thank you for looking up "that word" and stealing my affections. Each time you put your arms around me, I'm reminded you are here to stay as we learn to love each other more deeply with each new season of life. Thank you for protecting and providing for our family with your prayer life and wisdom.

For the most important "results" of our marriage—three daughters and one son—Kristin, Rob, Kandace, Kara, and our son-in-law, Rick (Bloomquist). We pray the blessings of Abraham over your lives, your spouses, both present and future. Follow Jesus with your whole heart, with your will, and in all your ways.

To Dallas Richard (lil' Ricky), our brand new grandson, born one month before we finished writing this book. We have already been praying for you and the grandchildren who will follow, praying for the spouse you will one day marry!

We have had two strong examples of parents committed to God and to their marriages. . .for life! (Bob and Beverly Crosby and David and Shirley Krist.) You all took your vows seriously, and we are *seriously* grateful for it. The impact of your choices continues to impact our families, for generations to come.

These are exciting days to be serving at Southeastern University (www.seu.edu). It is a privilege for us to teach, equip, and share life with such wonderful and motivated students, staff, faculty, and leadership. We pray God's best for each of our students and for those of you who one day choose to marry, that those unions will be powerfully blessed (Ephesians 3:20).

So glad to be a part of two wonderful teams in Tampa (Florida)—City Church Tampa and Q Commons. Urbanization is in full swing. Many people are moving to the great cities of the world, and God is raising up churches to *create kingdom culture* in those places! What an honor we share serving the kingdom of God where He has planted us.

Blythe Daniel, "our" literary agent—whether you know it or not, what helped us make the decision to take on this project was your enthusiasm and encouragement! Did Pam keep her parts "gritty" enough for you? Thank you for your impact on our lives. We count ourselves blessed to call you a friend.

A big thank-you to all the churches and ministries who have already invited us to teach on the will of a man and the way of a woman—from Gateway Church in Imlay City, Michigan, all the way to the *Salvemos a la Familia* (i.e., Save the Family) churches in Peru and Ecuador, and all the places in between. Your encouragement has helped grow the principle into couples' events and now into a book.

We appreciate the brave cadre of couples who met with to discuss these will and way principles. Thank you for sharing more about your lives and marriages: the East Coast Group—Jason and Hillary DeMeo, Ray and Gwen Allen, Angela and James An, and Myles and Sarah Schenk; and our West Coast Group and "soul" family—John and Jeannie Cochran and Gary and Sherry Cooley. Thanks for your candor! It helped. Uncle Jerry and Aunt Jolene, for opening your hearts and home to us, putting up with our final few hours of writing this manuscript.

Most of all, we are so grateful to Jesus, the truest and deepest source of our lives and marriage. He has revealed Himself as a passionate Bridegroom who left everything in order to give everything to His bride—that's us (Romans 5:8)! Help us learn to live Your will Your way.

Schedule an Event in Your Area with Robert and Pamela Crosby

TEAMING LIFE INITIATIVES
Speaking, Consulting, and Resources for:
Connecting—Collaboration—Community
Doing Life Together
at Home, Church, and Work

Contact info available at:
Teaminglife.com

Also, view videos and articles by Robert and Pamela Crosby
on *The Will of a Man and the Way of a Woman*

Follow us @teaminglife

ENDNOTES

1. Belinda Luscombe, "How to Stay Married," *Time*, July 13, 2016, 39.

2. Ibid., 38.

3. Ibid.

4. Ibid.

5. Marcel Proust, *Remembrance of Things Past*, transl. C. K. Scott-Moncrieff, New York: Random House, 1934, 169.

6. Luscombe, 40.

7. John Gottman's highly acclaimed research on marriage is documented in his books *The Seven Principles for Making Marriage Work: A Practical Guide from the Country's Foremost Relationship Expert* (New York: Harmony/Crown, 1999) and *What Makes Love Last?: How to Build Trust and Avoid Betrayal* (New York: Simon and Schuster, 2012).

8. "Connecting with Your Partner: An Introduction to Leading and Following in Salsa Dancing," SalsaDancingTips.com, accessed May 26, 2016, http://www.salsadancingtips.com/leading-following-technique.html.

9. John and Stasi Eldredge, *Love and War: Finding the Marriage You've Dreamed Of* (New York: Doubleday, 2009), 67.

10. Peter Opie and Iona Opie, *The Oxford Dictionary of Nursery Rhymes*, 2nd ed. (Oxford: Oxford University Press, 1997), 100–01.

11. "Statistics on the Father Absence Crisis in America," National Fatherhood Initiative. Fatherhood.org, accessed May 26, 2016, http://www.fatherhood.org/media/consequences-of-father-absence-statistics.

12. Brennan Manning, *The Importance of Being Foolish: How to Think Like Jesus* (New York: HarperOne, 2005), 57.

13. The full quote of this phrase on changing moods is drawn from one of our favorites by Lewis from *Mere Christianity* and is a key to maturity in marriage, in faith, and in life in general. Here it is in full:

> *Now Faith, in the sense in which I am here using the word, is the art of holding on to things your reason has once accepted, in spite of your changing moods. For moods will change, whatever view your reason takes. I know that by experience. Now that I am a Christian I do have moods in which the whole thing looks very improbable: but when I was an atheist I had moods in which Christianity looked terribly probable. This rebellion of your moods against your real self is going to come anyway. That is why Faith is such a necessary virtue:* unless you teach your moods "where they get off," *you can never be either a sound Christian or even a sound atheist, but just a creature dithering to and fro, with its beliefs really dependent on the weather and the state of its digestion. Consequently one must train the habit of Faith.*

From C. S. Lewis, *Mere Christianity* (New York: Touchstone, 1996), 125, emphasis mine.

14. Charles R. Swindoll, "Be Who You Are." *The Pastor's Blog* (blog), Insights for Living Ministries, accessed May 26, 2016, http://pastors.iflblog.com/2011/07/be-who-you-are/.

15. Anthony Campolo, *The Power Delusion: A Serious Call to Consider Jesus' Approach to Power* (Wheaton, IL: Victor Books, 1984), 11.

16. Robert Crosby, "The One Jesus Loves" (Nashville, TN: Nelson Books, 2014), 122.

17. John Gottman, *Why Marriages Succeed or Fail: And How You Can Make Yours Last* (New York: Simon & Schuster, 1994), 73.

18. Henry Cloud and John Townsend, *Safe People: How to Find Relationships That Are Good for You and Avoid Those That Aren't* (Grand Rapids, MI: Zondervan, 1996), 31.

19. Jessie Potter, quoted in Tom Ahern, "Search for Quality Called Key to Life," *The Milwaukee Sentinel*, October 24, 1981, accessed June 20, 2016, Google News Archive.

20. John Gottman, *The Man's Guide to Women: Scientifically Proven Secrets from the "Love Lab" about What Women Really Want* (New York: Rodale, 2016), 7, 10; emphasis mine.

21. Dee Brestin, *The Friendships of Women: The Beauty and Power of God's Plan for Us* (Colorado Springs: David C. Cook, 2008), 2.

22. Gary Smalley and John Trent, *The Language of Love* (Pomona, CA: Focus on the Family Publishing, 1988), 20.

23. Gottman, *Man's Guide to Women*, 10.

24. Ed Batista, "How to Not Fight with Your Spouse When You Get Home from Work," *Harvard Business Review*, April 12, 2016, accessed May 26, 2016, https://hbr.org/2016/04/how-to-not-fight-with-your-spouse-when-you-get-home-from-work.

25. Shiri Cohen, "Women Happier in Relationships When Men Feel Their Pain," American Psychological Association, March 5, 2012, accessed May 26, 2016, http://www.apa.org/news/press/releases/2012/03/women-happier.aspx.

26. Ibid.

27. Peggy Bert, "Positive and Negative Words," *Today's Christian Woman*, September 2008, accessed June 7, 2016, http://www.todayschristianwoman.com/articles/2008/september/7.26.html.

28. Gary Smalley, Twitter post, May 19, 2014, 7:46 a.m., accessed June 7, 2016, https://twitter.com/drgarysmalley/status/468402259554869249.

29. Dale Carnegie, *How to Win Friends and Influence People* (New York: Simon and Schuster, 1964), 55.

30. Dan and Kate Montgomery, *The Self Compass: Charting Your Personality in Christ* (Montecito, CA: Compass Works, 2010), 3. We also recommend other books by the Montgomerys, including *Christian Counseling That Really Works* and *Pastoral Counseling and Coaching*.

31. Lindsay Peterson, "Longtime Couples Get In Sync, In Sickness and In Health," NPR.com, May 22, 2016, accessed May 26, 2016, http://www.npr.org/sections/health-shots/2016/05/22/478826744/longtime-couples-get-in-sync-in-sickness-and-in-health.

32. Ibid.

33. George Cladis, *Leading the Team-Based Church* (San Francisco: Jossey-Bass, 1999), 4–5.

34. Gottman, *Man's Guide to Women*, 12.

35. Ibid.

36. Ibid., 7.

37. Eldredge, *Love and War*, 67.

38. Gottman, *Man's Guide to Women*, 12.

39. Deborah Tannen, *You Just Don't Understand: Men and Women in Conversation* (New York: William Morrow, 2007), 17.

40. Luscombe, 41.

41. Gottman, *Man's Guide to Women*, 109.

42. Gary Smalley, Erin Smalley, and Greg Smalley, *The Wholehearted Wife: 10 Keys to a More Loving Relationship* (Carol Stream, IL: Tyndale, 2014), 87.

43. Rodney Cooper, *Double Bind: Escaping the Contradictory*

Demands of Manhood (Grand Rapids, MI: Zondervan, 1996), 17.

44. *The Magic of Flight*, directed by Greg MacGillivray, narrated by Tom Selleck (Laguna Beach, CA: MacGillivray Freeman Films, 1996), DVD.

45. Eldredge, *Love and War*, 36.

46. Erma Bombeck, *Family—The Ties that Bind. . .and Gag!* (New York: Fawcett Books, 1988), 2.

47. Luscombe, 41.

48. Ibid.

49. Timothy and Kathy Keller, *The Meaning of Marriage: Facing the Complexities of Commitment with the Wisdom of God* (New York: Penguin, 2013), 32.

50. Robert E. Cooley, interview with the author, June 17, 2004, Burlington, MA.

51. Eldredge, *Love and War*, 180–81.

52. Gottman, *Man's Guide to Women*, 106.

53. Ibid., 7.

54. Ibid., 93–94.

55. Ibid., 106.

56. "Finish This Sentence: 'The Most Beautiful Sound in the World Is…'" *Reader's Digest*, accessed on June 7, 2016, http://www.rd.com/culture/finish-this-sentence-beautiful-sound/.

57. Charles R. Swindoll, "Giving is Godlike," *Insight for Today*, Insight.org, September 3, 2015, accessed on June 7, 2016, https://www.insight.org/resources/daily-devotional/individual/giving-is-godlike.

If You Liked This Book, You'll Also Like...

Jehova-Rapha: The God Who Heals
by Mary J. Nelson

Jehovah-Rapha: The God Who Heals features 72 comforting and encouraging meditations and stories based on healing scriptures—pointing readers to God, the Ultimate Healer. Written by author, speaker, pastor of prayer, and cancer survivor, Mary J. Nelson shares the Word without compromise, releases hope, and focuses on the heavenly Father's infinite love and grace.

Paperback / 978-1-63409-198-5 / $14.99

Dangerous Prayer by Cheri Fuller

Join gifted speaker and award-winning author, Cheri Fuller, as she illustrates—from Bible times to today—what happens when God's people pray dangerous prayers. Each of the 21 chapters is rooted in scripture and weaves together a beautiful tapestry of lives and kingdoms impacted through the power of prayer.

Paperback / 978-1-63409-115-2 / $14.99